Divine Connection

By Author

EVANGELIST INNOCENT

Unless otherwise noted, scriptures quoted are from the New King James Version of the Bible. Copyright © 1979, 1980, 1982, 1985 by Thomas Nelson Inc. Used by permission.

Text copyright © 2008 by Evangelist Innocent
All Rights Reserved
ISBN: 978-1-921698-50-7 (Print)
ISBN: 978-1-921698-51-4 (eBook)

All rights reserved. No part of this publication may be reproduced, stored in a retrieval system, or transmitted in any form or by any means, electronic, mechanical, photocopying, recording, or otherwise, without the prior written permission of the publisher and copyrighters.

CONTENTS

	Page
FORWARD	1
ACKNOWLEDGEMENTS	7
OPENING PRAYER	8
INTRODUCTION	9

CHAPTER 1
DIVINE CONNECTION 21
  Come To Me 25
    Restored 25
    Enlarge Your Commitment In God's Work 29
    Soul Winning 31
      1. Speak The Reality Of The Gospel 33
      2. Speak The Word Of Faith 34
      3. Speak Through Your Phone Or Internet 35
      4. Take Them To Dinner And Share The Word With Them 37
      5. Carry You Bible With You At All Time 38
      6. Speak What Is In The Bible 39
      7. Speak The Word To Anyone You See 40
      8. Do Not Be Afraid 42
      9. Speak What God Says 44
      10. Have The Compassion of Love 47
    Truthfulness 50
  Obedience 52
  New Life 54
  Nearer 56
  Eternity 57
  Co-Operate 62
  Testify 64
  Imitate 66

Original　　　　　　　　　　　　　　　　67
　　Narrow Gate　　　　　　　　　　　　　　69
　　　　The Worldly Gate　　(Wide Gate)　　71
　　　　The Heavenly Gate (Narrow Gate)　　77

CHAPTER 2
DOUBLE PORTION ANOINTING　　　　　81
　　Double Portion Anointing Can Make One
　　To Live A Long Life　　　　　　　　　　88
　　Double Portion Anointing Can Be Transformed
　　By The Anointing Oil　　　　　　　　　　88

CHAPTER 3　　　　　　　　　　　　　　　95
DO YOUR PART IN GOD'S WORK　　　　95

CHAPTER 4
JESUS AND THE SAMARITAN WOMAN　107
　　Zacchaeus And Jesus　　　　　　　　　109

CHAPTER 5
THE WOMAN WITH THE ISSUE OF BLOOD　115

CHAPTER 6
RAHAB AND THE TWO SPIES　　　　　125
　　Repent　　　　　　　　　　　　　　　　127
　　Abide　　　　　　　　　　　　　　　　132
　　Honour　　　　　　　　　　　　　　　136
　　Appointed Time　　　　　　　　　　　139
　　Believe　　　　　　　　　　　　　　　141

CHAPTER 7
LAZARUS COME FORTH　　　　　　　145
　　Prapyer For God's Blessing　　　　　　147
　　Prayer For God To Use You　　　　　　155

CHAPTER 8
ESTHER AND MORDECAI　　　　　　　157

CHAPTER 9
MY JOURNEY TO CHINA 167

CHAPTER 10
CORNELIUS AND APOSTLE PETER 177

CHAPTER 11
JOSEPH USED HIS GIFTS 185

CHAPTER 12
PAUL AND BARNABAS 195

CHAPTER 13
MY JOURNEY TO INDIA 201
   It Shall Come To Pass 208

CHAPTER 14
JESUS AND BLIND BARTIMAEUS 215

CHAPTER 15
HEALING 221
   Jesus Heals The Blind Man 227

CHAPTER 16
THE BENEFITS 233
   Wake Up 235
   Abide And Arise 237
   Testify 240
   Obedient 242
   Imitate 243
   Love 245
   Cross-Crowned 246
   Hope 248
      Honour 249
      Obedient 250
      Unbelief 252
      Righteousness 253

EPILOGUE **255**
   Prayer For Obedience   256
   Prayer For Exposure In The Ministry   258
   Prayer For Barnabas Of This End Time   259

ABOUT THE AUTHOR   **261**

LIST OF OTHER BOOKS WRITTEN BY THE AUTHOR   **265**

FORWARD

༄༅

Our Divine Connection

We are to abide in Christ and be filled with the Spirit. What we do, we do in Him, not by our strength or wisdom, but by abiding in Him. To be born again is to be filled with His Spirit. We are spirit, soul and body, but beyond that, we are to receive the in-filling of the Holy Spirit. That is what makes us holy, His Spirit, not our own. We can try to be holy but we will fail on our own strength. When God touches an individual, it is a divine touch from heaven. After this happens, there should be changes that occur in one's life. They are to move and go on into maturity in the Lord. The work of the Holy Spirit is to convince, convict, counsel, guide and comfort.

These are just a few things that God would like to do for us. We have a will and we either choose to be led by His Spirit, or we refuse Him. In this life we need help, the Holy Spirit is our helper, he knows what we have needs of. If we pray and are led by

God's Spirit, we are in submission and will go in the direction that God would desire us to go.

He looks for willing and submitted vessels. When first coming to Christ, I was told I was being brainwashed. I do not know if that is how it was for any of you out there. But the enemy tried all ways to put fear in me about God and coming to Christ. I came to Him because I desperately needed help. I was on a downward spiral towards hell and the grave. At a young age of 17, I was tired of living and being on this earth. I did not know I was being controlled by the spirit of suicide. I just wasn't making it, nor could I handle what was happening around me. Jesus came to me and witnessed to me through a very young man, I accepted the Good News and baptized by the Holy Spirit, it was a very quick work, as the Lord knew I needed major help. By the way, that young boy became my husband and 30 years or so later, we are still being led by His Spirit, and still need His help today. We are always to be growing in the Lord, and seeking Him for the plans that He has made for us. We are always to be growing in God. No matter how old we are, there are always new opportunities and we are to move forward in them. We are being prepared for life with Him when we will rule and reign with Christ.

For now, we need the Holy Spirit to propel us into the plans that God desires for us to follow. We are married, but still, an individual as we will give an account for what we do in this life. I cannot say to God when I stand before Him, that I did everything to help my husband become the man that he should be when He had given to me gifts and talents that I should have accomplished something also. I will have to give an account for what He had given to me in this life also.

We are to compliment each other not control as we each will give an account for what we do in this life. Through the Holy Spirit, we have had an impartation of the very nature of God. He was given to impart to us what is needed to accomplish what we need in this life. The gifts and callings of God are for this time and without them, we are able to accomplish nothing. Even this email every morning is done by God's spirit working through me. I make many mistakes, misspelled words, phrases that might not make sense at times or maybe that make one angry, but nevertheless, I am to be obedient to do what He has given me to do. It is my hope that it is a help and a blessing, but at times it might not be.

The Holy Spirit presents and proves what the moral presence of God is. He writes on the tables of our hearts, what pleases God or what does not. He is what divinely connects us to the Father, and he was sent from Jesus to help us in this life. He is the wind, or breath of God, that imparts to us His wisdom and knowledge. We sure need it today. God gives us gifts and talents for us to use for Him. If we use them for anything else, we may find ourselves being confused or led astray. We need the gift of discernment today, and God does want to give this gift. We are to examine ourselves to see if we are in the faith. So it all starts with us each individually.

Not by Might, nor by Power, but by His Spirit......

What Do You Need Today?

As I close this letter, I feel compelled to ask that question. To show that God does exist in this life, we are to move forward in God and to accomplish what He has given us to do. Many of you reading this have callings and are to be moving, demonstrating God to all who you are led to. It is our prayer that you are not trying to do it on your own strength but to be empowered and equipped in God for this mighty task that you are to accomplish. You are called a minister; His minister. He knows what you need before you even ask, but you are to ask and then receive as God wants to show Himself through your life and calling. People will either see the Spirit of Christ in you or you. We want all to see God as we cannot take the glory for anything. God is looking for submitted and willing vessels, so we are to submit this morning and yield to His Spirit. Someone will be coming to Christ today. It will be because we are tools in the Lord's hands. Bless God and bless you as we look together to accomplish what is next, even if it is today. Amen.

In Covenant Keeping,

REVD. ALAGBAOSO ELEAZAR
SENIOR PASTOR

GRACE CHRISTIAN ASSEMBLY

LAGOS, NIGERIA.

ACKNOWLEDGEMENTS

༺༻

I want to thank God Almighty for giving me the privilege, the unction and the power to write this book. I give Him all the praise and adoration.

May His name be highly lifted up, in the name of Jesus Christ. I also thank Him for the other books that I have written, and more to be written. I believe every man and woman reading this book will not be a double minded person.

I want to assure you, this book was not written by my own power but by the power of the Holy Spirit. I hope after reading this book, may your life be transformed.

May God bless you and keep you always, in Jesus mighty name.

OPENING PRAYER

※

Shall We Pray

Forever O LORD, Your Word is indestructible. I ask Thee O LORD, to give me the grace to read this book and be blessed through it. I ask Thee O LORD, to expose me in the ministry you have called me to hold. I asked Thee O LORD, after reading this book, let my weakness turns to strength. I ask Thee O LORD, to reverse every problem that I am passing through and be restored. Transform me O LORD.

In the name of Jesus. Amen.

Before reading this book, for 5 minutes, ask God what you want Him to do for you.

"Ask, and it will be given to you; seek, and you will find; knock, and it will be opened to you.
(Matthew 7:7)

INTRODUCTION

༝༠

Beloved, if you want to have a divine connection with God, take note that many will be looking down on you.

> No longer do I call you servants, for a servant does not know what his master is doing; but I have called you friends, for all things that I heard from My Father I have made known to you. You did not choose Me, but I chose you and appointed you that you should go and bear fruit, and that your fruit should remain, that whatever you ask the Father in My name He may give you. These things I command you, that you love one another. "If the world hates you, you know that it hated Me before it hated you. If you were of the world, the world would love its own. Yet because you are not of the world, but I chose you out of the world, therefore the world hates you. Remember the word that I said to you, 'A servant is not greater than his master.' If they persecuted Me, they will also

persecute you. If they kept My word, they will keep yours also.

(John 15:15-20)

Remember that our Lord Jesus Christ was criticized by many. Still, He carried the cross to fulfil the Scripture. Likewise, His apostles also were criticized. But they did not give up.

And they agreed with him, and when they had called for the apostles and beaten them, they commanded that they should not speak in the name of Jesus, and let them go. So they departed from the presence of the council, rejoicing that they were counted worthy to suffer shame for His name. And daily in the temple, and in every house, they did not cease teaching and preaching Jesus as the Christ.

(Acts 5:40-42)

Jeremiah was also criticized and went through tremendous trials and temptation in so many occasions. Jeremiah 37:13-21 says, "And when he was in the Gate of Benjamin, a captain of the guard was there whose name was Irijah the son of Shelemiah, the son of Hananiah; and he seized Jeremiah the prophet, saying, "You are defecting to the Chaldeans!" Then Jeremiah said, "False! I am not defecting to the Chaldeans." But he did not listen to him. So Irijah seized Jeremiah and brought him to the princes. Therefore the princes were angry with Jeremiah, and they struck him and put him in prison in the house of Jonathan the scribe. For they had made that the prison. *When Jeremiah entered the dungeon and the cells, and Jeremiah had remained there many days,* then Zedekiah the king sent and took him out. The king asked him secretly in his house, and said, "Is there any word from the LORD?" And Jeremiah said, "There is." Then he said, "You shall be delivered into the hand of the king of Babylon!" Moreover, Jeremiah said to King Zedekiah, "What offence have I committed against you, against your servants, or against this people, that you have put me in prison? Where now are your prophets who prophesied to you, saying, 'The king of Babylon will not come against you or against this land'? Therefore please hear now, O my lord the king. Please, let my petition be accepted before you, and do not make me return to the house of Jonathan the scribe, lest I die there." *Then Zedekiah the king commanded that they should commit Jeremiah to the court of the prison, and that they should give him daily a piece of bread from the bakers' street, until all the bread in the city was gone. Thus Jeremiah remained in the court of the prison."*

The Word of God to Jeremiah, on behalf of the people of Israel says in Jeremiah 40:2-4 that they would have to surrender to Nebuchadnezzar and it came to pass. Likewise, Nehemiah also went through tremendous crisis but at the appointed time, he accomplished his assignment for the rebuilding of the walls of Jerusalem.

Nehemiah 6:1-3 says, "Now it happened when Sanballat, Tobiah, Geshem the Arab, and the rest of our enemies heard that I had rebuilt the wall, and that there were no breaks left in it though at that time I had not hung the doors in the gates that Sanballat and Geshem sent to me, saying, "Come, let us meet together among the villages in the plain of Ono." But they thought to do me harm. So I sent messengers to them, saying, "I am doing a great work, so that I cannot come down. Why should the work cease while I leave it and go down to you?"

To make a long story short, listen to what Scripture says in Nehemiah 7:1-2, "Then it was, when the wall was built and I had hung the doors, when the gatekeepers, the singers, and the Levites had been appointed, that I gave the charge of Jerusalem to my brother Hanani, and Hananiah the leader of the citadel, for he was a faithful man and feared God more than many."

For to me, to live is Christ, and to die is gain.
(Philippians 1:21)

Rahab risked her life when she hid the two spies. Joshua 2:1-4 says, "Now Joshua the son of Nun sent out two men from Acacia Grove to spy secretly, saying, 'Go, view the land, especially Jericho.' So they went, and came to the house of a harlot named Rahab, and lodged there. And it was told the king of Jericho, saying, 'Behold, men have come here tonight from the children of Israel to search out the country.' So the king of Jericho sent to Rahab, saying, 'Bring out the men who have come to you, who have entered your house, for they have come to search out all the country.' Then the woman took the two men and hid them. So she said, 'Yes, the men came to me, but I did not know where they were from.'

The bible tells us that because of what Rahab did for the two spies and the covenant she made with them she and her family were saved and allowed to dwell with the people of Israel.

Another person who did something spectacular was Mordecai. He did not bow down to the enemy of God's people. The bible tells us in Esther 3:4-6, *"Now it happened, when they spoke to him daily* and he would not listen to them, that they told it to Haman, to see whether Mordecai's words would stand; for Mordecai had told them that he was a Jew. When Haman saw that Mordecai did not bow or pay him homage, Haman was filled with wrath. But he disdained to lay hands on Mordecai alone, for they had told him of the people of Mordecai. Instead, Haman sought to destroy all the Jews who were throughout the whole kingdom of Ahasuerus — the people of Mordecai."

Even when the decree has been made to destroy all the Jews, still Mordecai did not bow down to Haman. Esther 5:9 says, "So Haman went out that day joyful and with a glad heart; but when Haman saw Mordecai in the king's gate, and that he did not stand or tremble before him, he was filled with indignation against Mordecai."

If you want to have a divine connection with God, Jesus said in Matthew 10:22, "And you will be hated by all for My name's sake. But he who endures to the end will be saved."

In Esther 10:2-3 it says, "Now all the acts of his power and his might, and the account of the greatness of Mordecai, to which the king advanced him, are they not written in the book of the chronicles of the kings of Media and Persia? For Mordecai, the

Jew was second to King Ahasuerus, and was great among the Jews and well received by the multitude of his brethren, seeking the good of his people and speaking peace to all his countrymen."

I hope you know the story about Stephen. He was stoned by the multitude because he was preaching the gospel of Jesus Christ.

> When they heard these things they were cut to the heart, and they gnashed at him with their teeth. But he, being full of the Holy Spirit, gazed into heaven and saw the glory of God, and Jesus standing at the right hand of God, and said, "Look! I see the heavens opened and the Son of Man standing at the right hand of God!" Then they cried out with a loud voice, stopped their ears, and ran at him with one accord; and they cast him out of the city and stoned him. And the witnesses laid down their clothes at the feet of a young man named Saul.
>
> (Acts 7:54-58)

We have read how Stephen saw Jesus standing at the right hand of God the Father. Honestly, divine connection is the confirmation of God's word and purpose which He has set for us.

But Saul increased all the more in strength, and confounded the Jews who dwelt in Damascus, proving that this Jesus is the Christ. Now after many days were past, the Jews plotted to kill him. But their plot became known to Saul. And they watched the gates day and night, to kill him. Then the disciples took him by night and let him down through the wall in a large basket.

(Acts 9:22-25)

But Barnabas took him and brought him to the apostles. And he declared to them how he had seen the Lord on the road, and that He had spoken to him, and how he had preached boldly at Damascus in the name of Jesus.

(Acts 9: 27)

We have seen that Barnabas was the person God used to expose Saul (who later became Paul) to the apostles. According to the Scripture in Acts 9:28-31 "And when Saul had come to Jerusalem, he tried to join the disciples; but they were all afraid of him, and did not believe that he was a disciple. But Barnabas took him and brought him to the apostles. And he declared to them how he had seen the Lord on the road, and that He had spoken to him, and how he had preached boldly at Damascus in the name of Jesus. So he was with them at Jerusalem, coming in and going out. And he spoke boldly in the name of the Lord Jesus and disputed against the Hellenists, but they attempted to kill him. When the brethren found out, they brought him down to Caesarea and sent him out to Tarsus."

If you want to have a divine connection with God, follow the example of Barnabas in this end time. However, today many are not willing to expose others that God has called into the ministry. Rather, they will do things according to human mentality. Beloved, are you a Barnabas of this end time? I have a story to share with you.

I know of a preacher in my hometown, who was willing to die for the gospel of Jesus Christ. He was not given a chance to preach the gospel in the church he was serving, even though he knew that he was called to preach. When I discovered about it, I brought him to one of the biggest markets in my hometown to preach because, in the marketplace, they have fellowship meetings in each of the section of the marketplace. So, he became known to them because God inspired me to do so and he was blessed there. Whatever he was lacking in, God provided, through the businessmen in the marketplace.

Beloved, Apostle Paul said in 1 Corinthians 3:6-7, "I planted, Apollos watered, but God gave the increase. So then neither he who plants is anything, nor he who waters, but God who gives the increase."

Because the foolishness of God is wiser than men, and the weakness of God is stronger than men.
(1 Corinthians 1:25)

We should give others the opportunity to be exposed in the ministry wherever necessary and if it is the will of God. Even though you have not yet been exposed, continue to be faithful to God and obey God in whatever He told you to do. King Ahashuerus, the king of Persia, chose Esther who was a Jew and the niece of Mordecai to be his queen. God used Esther to deliver the people of Israel from Haman's plot to annihilate them. She delivered Mordecai from Haman's wicked plan to hang him, by exposing Haman's plan to the king.

So they hanged Haman on the gallows that he had prepared for Mordecai. Then the king's wrath subsided.
(Esther 7:10)

What do you think would happen if Esther had refused to intercede for the people of Israel, before the king? God could still use someone else to deliver the people of Israel but it does not mean that Esther would be saved from being killed also because she was also a Jew. However, she obeyed her calling and because of this, the people of Israel were delivered from Haman's plan to annihilate them. She also told the king about Mordecai and how he was related to her. Today, in the various churches of this end time, there are many who have been assisting some pastors are not given the privilege to preach while they are called to be there.

> This wisdom I have also seen under the sun, and it seemed great to me: There was a little city with few men in it; and a great king came against it, besieged it, and built great snares around it. Now there was found in it a poor wise man, and he by his wisdom delivered the city. Yet no one remembered that same poor man.
> (Ecclesiastes 9:13-15)

I discovered that the reason why many preachers or believers are not willing to introduce others in the ministry is because they only want only themselves to be noticed. They also want others to see them as the head over all. Beloved, it does not work like that.

> Yet it shall not be so among you; but whoever desires to become great among you, let him

be your servant. And whoever desires to be first among you, let him be your slave—just as the Son of Man did not come to be served, but to serve, and to give His life a ransom for many.

(Matthew 20:26-28)

We have seen what Jesus said. Whatever name or position we are bearing, whether a bishop or an apostle or a teacher or any other position; we are servants of the Most High God. I believe at Judgement Day, God will not call us by the title we bear but He will want us to give an account of what we have done for Him while you were living on the earth and He will reward you accordingly.

For if I do this willingly, I have a reward; but if against my will, I have been entrusted with a stewardship.
(1 Corinthians 9:17)

I have fought the good fight, I have finished the race, I have kept the faith. Finally, there is laid up for me the crown of righteousness, which the Lord, the righteous Judge, will give to me on that Day, and not to me only but also to all who have loved His appearing.

(2 Timothy 4:7-8)

CHAPTER 1

DIVINE CONNECTION

৵৶

What does it mean to have a divine connection? It is the God given grace to obtain favour from God. It is the confirmation of God's calling in our lives. It is not by our might or power that enables us to receive divine connection but it is only by the power of the Holy Spirit. It is the divine proof that God's calling in our lives came to pass - a God-given right. It is the ability to make us believe that the authority comes directly from God rather than from men.

For example, the Samaritan woman who had five husbands and was dating another man was connected to meet Jesus at Jacob's well. Probably, God has called her into the ministry but because of the devil's manipulation, her calling did not come to pass until she met Jesus at Jacob's well. Imagine that, she was the one who went as far as to testify to those in the city of Samaria that she has seen the Messiah.

And many of the Samaritans of that city believed in Him because of the word of the woman who testified, "He told me all that I ever did."
(John 4:39)

Beloved, know that God is real and not a myth. Divine connection is a testimony in our lives, which confirms our calling to the ministry, to preach the gospel to those who do not know about Jesus Christ, who is The Way, The Truth and The Life.

Now he was ruddy, with bright eyes, and good-looking. And the LORD said, "Arise, anoint him; for this is the one!" Then Samuel took the horn of oil and anointed him in the midst of his brothers; and the Spirit of the LORD came upon David from that day forward.
(1 Samuel 16:12-13)

Although David was just a ruddy young lad, yet God used Samuel to anoint David to be the next king. Later, David was the one God used to defeat Goliath. He went through trials and tribulations for many years but at the appointed time, he became king of Israel. Remember that David wrote in one of his Psalms that those who put their trust in God shall be as Mount Zion which cannot be removed but abides forever.

When you put your trust in God and begin to live a righteous life, you will not lose hope even though many may look down on you because he who endures to the end shall be saved.

I challenge you that God will see you through, in Jesus mighty name. There was a great man of God named Oyedepo who struggled to make it when he first started his ministry but he continued to stay faithful to God. One day, God told him to go to America to meet the late Archbishop Idahosa who blessed him with money for his journey and prayer.

When Bishop Oyedepo returned from America, God spoke to him to give all the money he has brought back from America, to the man of God who had sponsored him to go to America. He obeyed what God told him to do. The man of God who sponsored him told him to march on the money and then told him that he will never lack all the days of his life.

Do you know God has blessed him and his ministry, from being a pastor of a church that was a make-shift structure capable of only shading them from the sun, which it was built of woven grass, on a two-plot leased landed property to the world renowned Faith Tabernacle with a 50,000 seat sanctuary? It is reputed to be one of the largest church auditoriums in the world. He also has a private jet to fly him to the various states in Nigeria and to other countries to preach the gospel.

Honestly, ever since I became a believer of Christ, I have never seen anyone who said that he or she who is living in faith ever complained that God has failed them.

Beloved, if you are willing to have a divine connection with God, understanding the following comprehensive meaning of CONNECTIONS could help you reach that goal.

C   Come to Me
O   Obedience
N   New Life
N   Nearer
E   Eternity
C   Co-operate
T   Testify
I   Imitate
O   Original
N   Narrow Gate

COME TO ME

Come to Me, all you who labour and are heavy laden, and I will give you rest.
(Matthew 11:28)

Beloved, the word of God says that God will give us rest, which simply means:

R   Restored
E   Enlarge Your Commitment In God's Work
S   Soul Winning
T   Truthfulness

Restored

Beloved, as you march forward and you are passing through trials and temptation, continue to trust in God because He will definitely restore your circumstances. When God restores you, you know that you have passed the examination. It will be the time when God will manifest His power in you. For example, the bible tells us that Rahab risked her life when she hid the two spies sent by Joshua to spy on Jericho. Beloved, do you think that it was easy for a woman to take such a risk as Rahab did? If the king discovered that she had hidden the two spies, she would be severely punished or even be put to death.

Now before they lay down, she came up to them on the roof, and said to the men: "I know that the LORD has given you the land, that the terror of you has fallen on us, and that all the inhabitants of the land are fainthearted because of you. For we have heard how the LORD dried up the water of the Red Sea for you when you came out of Egypt, and what you did to the two kings of the Amorites who were on the other side of the Jordan, Sihon and Og, whom you utterly destroyed. And as soon as we heard these things, our hearts melted; neither did there remain any more courage in anyone because of you, for the LORD your God, He is God in heaven above and on earth beneath. Now therefore, I beg you, swear to me by the LORD, since I have shown you kindness, that you also will show kindness to my father's house, and give me a true token, and spare my father, my mother, my brothers, my sisters, and all that they have, and deliver our lives from death." So the men answered her, "Our lives for yours, if none of you tell this business of ours. And it shall be, when the LORD has given us the land, that we will deal kindly and truly with you."

(Joshua 2:8-14)

Joshua led the people of Israel to march around Jericho as God has instructed. On the seventh day, as they marched around the city seven times, the priest blew the trumpets and the people shouted. It happened when the people shouted with a great shout, the wall of the city fell down flat. Then the people went in and took the city.

> But Joshua had said to the two men who had spied out the country, "Go into the harlot's house, and from there bring out the woman and all that she has, as you swore to her." And the young men who had been spies went in and brought out Rahab, her father, her mother, her brothers, and all that she had. So they brought out all her relatives and left them outside the camp of Israel. But they burned the city and all that was in it with fire. Only the silver and gold, and the vessels of bronze and iron, they put into the treasury of the house of the LORD. And Joshua spared Rahab the harlot, her father's household, and all that she had. So she dwells in Israel to this day,

because she hid the messengers whom Joshua sent to spy out Jericho.

(Joshua 6:22-26)

We have seen how God restored Rahab's life by connecting her to the people of God. Today, the descendants of Rahab still exist in Israel.

Salmon begot Boaz by Rahab, Boaz begot Obed by Ruth, Obed begot Jesse, and Jesse begot David the king.

(Matthew 1:5-6)

Therefore, we cannot fold our hands and expect God to expose us in the ministry. I believe that we should be willing to risk our lives, for His namesake.

When they had called for the apostles and beaten them, they commanded that they should not speak in the name of Jesus, and let them go. So they departed from the presence of the council, rejoicing that they were counted worthy to suffer shame for His name. And daily in the temple, and in every house, they did not cease teaching and preaching Jesus as the Christ.

(Acts 5:40-42)

If you want to have a divine connection with God, know this that if it requires that we should lose our lives for His namesake, then we should be willing to do so and wait for His manifestation to take place.

Enlarge Your Commitment In God's Work

Beloved, I challenge you when you enlarge your commitment in God's work; God will surely expose you and bless you in every area of your life. When I was doing missionary work in Libya, I saw how God was leading me. I did not know anyone in Libya but because of my commitment to His work, God used a pastor in Libya to accommodate me and to sponsor my trip to Egypt. Therefore, when we put our effort in the things of God, He will never fail us in every area of our lives. Even when I travelled to Singapore, India, China, Malaysia, Thailand and other countries, God blessed me by His grace. Honestly, I did not know anyone when I went to those countries for the first time. Why did God bless me in the countries I travelled to; where I did not know anyone there? It is because I was not looking for a job that will pay me a salary every month. There is nothing wrong in getting a job which pays you a monthly salary but let the will of God be done.

Also I heard the voice of the Lord, saying: "Whom shall I send, and who will go for Us?" Then I said, "Here am I! Send me."

(Isaiah 6:8)

When God tells you to go to any country to preach the gospel, obey Him and start preaching the word wherever you are. Just speak the word of faith. There are many who do not believe that there is God. You who have come to believe in God and have received His gift of salvation, what do you do when you see those who do not know Jesus?

According to the Scripture in 2 Timothy 4:2 it says, "Preach the word! Be ready in season and out of season. Convince, rebuke, exhort, with all long suffering and teaching."

When we obey God and preach His Word in season and out of season, our Holy God will not fail us, in Jesus name. Many are saying that from year to year, God has not blessed them. Why are they not experiencing God's blessing? It is because they are afraid to speak out the reality of the Word of God. If you want to have a divine connection with God, see what the Scripture says in 1 Corinthians 9:16-17 *"For if I preach the gospel, I have nothing to boast of, for necessity is laid upon me; yes, woe is me if I do not preach the gospel! For if I do this willingly, I have a reward; but if against my will, I have been entrusted with a stewardship."*

Soul Winning

The fruit of the righteous is a tree of life, and he who wins souls is wise.

(Proverbs 11:30)

Beloved, if you are willing to have a divine connection with God, be part of soul winning for the kingdom of God. Today, there are many workers in the church but what about working outside the church premises? Do people think about it? There are two types of calling, the universal calling, which is part-timers and ecclesiastical calling, which is full-timers. Even though you may be a business-man, let me tell you that you will have to give an account of your stewardship to God on Judgement Day, according to the name you are bearing. So be willing to be a part of soul winning because Paul said that as many as were baptized into Christ Jesus, were also baptized into His death and resurrection. Beloved, take note when you become a born again Christian, the mark of Jesus is upon you.

From now on let no one trouble me, for I bear in my body the marks of the Lord Jesus.

(Galatians 6:17)

Fear not but prove to God that you are faithful to Him because you are His. Let me tell you, your righteousness and holiness will not make God expose you if you are not winning souls for Him. Yes, we are to live in righteousness, which means having a right standing before God, but how can you say that you are living a righteous life without being a part of soul winning?

Take note, soul winning is the ability and the vehicle that will make God to expose us in every predicament. It is the greatest task God has given to us to carry out and it is important to know that each one of us must be part of soul winning. Many children have gone astray because their Christian parents are not preaching the Word to them. However, their parents work very hard so that their children can go to the best schools so that their children can graduate and obtain their PhDs.

There is nothing wrong in having a PHD but God's time is always the best. It is of no use for someone to graduate and obtained his PHD but died one day and he ended up in hell fire because he was not a born again Christian.

What can we do to be part of soul winning? They are:

1. Speak the reality of the Word of God
2. Speak the Word of Faith
3. Speak through your phone or internet
4. Take them to dinner and share the Word with them
5. Carry your bible with you at all times
6. Speak what is in the bible
7. Speak the Word to anyone you see
8. Do not be afraid
9. Speak what God says
10. Have the compassion of love

1. Speak The Reality Of The Gospel

What then shall we say to these things? If God is for us, who can be against us?
(Romans 8:31)

Do you know that as many as received Him that He gave the power to become the children of God and we can do all things through Christ who strengthened us? It is not about your name or your kindness or your power. All that you have to do is to release the Word of God, based on the bible and leave the rest to God. Honestly, many are ashamed to speak the fact of the gospel. Many are afraid of what people will say about them. But let me tell you, if people do not criticize you, you have not started your journey yet.

Remember that Jesus was criticized on many occasions. The scripture in Mathew 12 says, "Now when the Pharisees heard it they said, "This fellow does not cast out demons except by Beelzebub, the ruler of the demons." Jesus knew their thoughts and said to them: "Every kingdom divided against itself is brought to desolation, and every city or house divided against itself will not stand. If Satan casts out Satan, he is divided against himself. How then will his kingdom stand?"

2. Speak The Word Of Faith
So then, faith comes by hearing, and hearing by the word of God.
(Romans 10:17)

Beloved, faith without work is dead and faith move with action. Faith is the ability to do mighty things for God. Faith is the vehicle that will bring us into His prominence. Faith is the substance of things hope for, evidence of things not seen. Without faith, we cannot become followers of Jesus Christ. It is by faith that we are saved in Christ. Faith moves mountain. By faith, we preach the gospel. By faith, we are more than conquerors. By faith, God will make a way when there seems to be no way. By faith, we possess our possession. By faith, we speak the reality of the gospel.

For we walk by faith, not by sight.
(2 Corinthians 5: 7)

3. Speak Through Your Phone Or Internet

Preach the word! Be ready in season and out of season. Convince, rebuke, exhort, with all long suffering and teaching. For the time will come when they will not endure sound doctrine, but according to their own desires, because they have itching ears, they will heap up for themselves teachers; and they will turn their ears away from the truth, and be turned aside to fables. But you be watchful in all things, endure afflictions, do the work of an evangelist, fulfill your ministry.
(2 Timothy 4:2-5)

Today, many are invited to speak the word of God through the television and internet. Honestly, many are being saved through the preaching of the Word through this media. I have listened to the preaching of many great men and women of God through the internet and it has blessed me a lot. No man on earth can dispute the gospel of Jesus Christ. From generation to generation, the gospel shall continue even if a law may be given to stop the preaching of the gospel.

According to the Scripture in Acts 12:1-6 says, "Now about that time Herod the king stretched out his hand to harass some from the church. Then he killed James the brother of John with the sword. And because he saw that it pleased the Jews, he proceeded further to seize Peter also. Now it was during the Days of Unleavened Bread. So when he had arrested him, he put him in prison and delivered him to four squads of soldiers to keep him, intending to bring him before the people after Passover. Peter was therefore kept in prison, but constant prayer was offered to God for him by the church. And when Herod was about to bring him out, that night Peter was sleeping, bound with two chains between two soldiers; and the guards before the door were keeping the prison." Verse 11, "And when Peter had come to himself, he said, "Now I know for certain that the Lord has sent His angel, and has delivered me from the hand of Herod and from all the expectation of the Jewish people."

Peter went to other places and preached the gospel to the people there until the day Herod died. In verse 17, "But motioning to them with his hand to keep silent, he declared to them how the Lord had brought him out of the prison. And he said, "Go, tell these things to James and to the brethren." And he departed and went to another place." Verse 21:24 says, "So on a set day Herod, arrayed in royal apparel, sat on his throne and gave an oration to them. And the people kept shouting, 'The voice of a god and not of a man!' Then immediately an angel of the Lord struck him, because he did not give glory to God. And he was eaten by worms and died. But the word of God grew and multiplied."

4. Take Them To Dinner And Share The Word With Them

And we know that all things work together for good to those who love God, to those who are the called according to His purpose.

(Romans 8:28)

Today, many are more interested to go to dinner and speak about earthly business instead of in the things of God. There is nothing wrong in speaking about your business, but God's time is always the best. I have spoken to many unbelievers about the gospel of Jesus in restaurants or café. I bought them food and share the gospel with them and then they accepted Jesus as their Lord and Saviour. Remember, Paul said, that if you do this willingly, you have a reward.

Now this I do for the gospel's sake, that I may be partaker of it with you. Do you not know that those who run in a race all run, but one receives the prize? Run in such a way that you may obtain it. And everyone who competes for the prize is temperate in all things. Now they do it to obtain a perishable crown, but we for an imperishable crown.
(1 Corinthians 9:23-25)

5. Carry You Bible With You At All Time
Beloved, remember that the Word of God is living and powerful, sharper than any two-edged sword, piercing even to the division of soul and spirit, and of joints and marrow, and is a discerner of the thoughts and intents of the heart.
(Hebrews 4:12)

One day I met a friend somewhere and we were sharing the Word of God. I shared with him a Scripture in the bible and he wanted to see if what I was saying is the truth. I had my bible with me at that time. So I opened the bible and showed him where it is written in the bible. He believed and he began to bless me financially. So, every believer should carry his bible in season and out of season.

Be sober, be vigilant; because your adversary the devil walks about like a roaring lion, seeking whom he may devour.
(1 Peter 5:8)

6. Speak What Is In The Bible

Beloved, we should speak the reality of the gospel.

This Book of the Law shall not depart from your mouth, but you shall meditate in it day and night, that you may observe to do according to all that is written in it. For then you will make your way prosperous, and then you will have good success.
(Joshua 1:8)

If you want to have a divine connection with God, know that when we speak the true gospel of Jesus Christ, honestly, God will appear to us as He appeared to Apostle Paul in Acts.

But the following night the Lord stood by him and said, "Be of good cheer, Paul; for as you have testified for Me in Jerusalem, so you must also bear witness at Rome."
(Acts 23:11)

We have seen how Jesus appeared to Apostle Paul telling him what He wanted him to do. So, when we are obedient to God, it shall be well with us. Ever since God has called me into the ministry, I always try to speak the reality of the gospel to anybody that may come along my way. I discovered that when we do this, our lives will be saved. Jesus said in Matthew 5, *"You are the salt of the earth; but if the salt loses its flavour, how shall it be seasoned? It is then good for nothing but to be thrown out and trampled underfoot by men. "You are the light of the world. A city that is set on a hill cannot be hidden. Nor do they light a lamp and put it under a basket, but on a lampstand, and it gives light to all who are in the house. Let your light so shine before men, that they may see your good works and glorify your Father in heaven."*

7. Speak The Word To Anyone You See

Apostle Paul said in 1 Corinthians 9, "For though I am free from all men, I have made myself a servant to all, that I might win the more; and to the Jews I became as a Jew, that I might win Jews; to those who are under the law, as under the law, that I might win those who are under the law; to those who are without law, as without law (not being without law toward God, but under law toward Christ, that I might win those who are without law; to the weak I became as weak, that I might win the weak. I have become all things to all men, that I might by all means save some. Now this I do for the gospel's sake, that I may be partaker of it with you.

Do you not know that those who run in a race all run, but one receives the prize? Run in such a way that you may obtain it. And everyone who competes for the prize is temperate in all things. Now they do it to obtain a perishable crown, but we for an imperishable crown. Therefore I run thus: not with uncertainty. Thus I fight: not as one who beats the air. But I discipline my body and bring it into subjection, lest, when I have preached to others, I myself should become disqualified."

Beloved, we should not discriminate others because of their colour. Today, many are holding fellowship meant only for their family members. If an outsider tries to join the fellowship, he or she would not be permitted to enter. 1 John 3:15-18 says, "Whoever hates his brother is a murderer, and you know that no murderer has eternal life abiding in him. By this, we know love, because He laid down His life for us. And we also ought to lay down our lives for the brethren. But whoever has this world's goods, and sees his brother in need, and shuts up his heart from him, how does the love of God abide in him? My little children, let us not love in word or in tongue, but in deed and in truth."

We should welcome anyone we see. Even though that person was a murderer, we should welcome him. Remember that Saul, who later changed his name to Paul, was a murderer who persecuted the Christians before his encounter with Jesus. Acts 7:58 says, *"and they cast him out of the city and stoned him. And the witnesses laid down their clothes at the feet of a young man named Saul."* However, when God arrested him, he became born again and he began to preach the gospel. God used Barnabas to introduce Paul to the apostles.

8. Do Not Be Afraid

The fear of the LORD is clean, enduring forever; the judgments of the LORD are true and righteous altogether.

(Psalm 19:9)

Beloved, Apostle Paul said in 2 Timothy 1:6-10, "Therefore I remind you to stir up the gift of God which is in you through the laying on of my hands. For God has not given us a spirit of fear, but of power and of love and of a sound mind.

Therefore do not be ashamed of the testimony of our Lord, nor of me His prisoner, but share with me in the sufferings for the gospel according to the power of God, who has saved us and called us with a holy calling, not according to our works, but according to His own purpose and grace which was given to us in Christ Jesus before time began, but has now been revealed by the appearing of our Saviour Jesus Christ, who has abolished death and brought life and immortality to light through the gospel."

If you want to have a divine connection with God, just release the word to the person even though he may be a killer, speak with the love of Jesus Christ. I have a testimony to share with you. There was a man who used to smoke cocaine and Indian hemp. One day a pastor came to his house and released the word of faith to him. Honestly speaking, that man did not have peace of mind since the day, the pastor released the Word of God to him. One day, the man came to the church where the pastor was preaching. He testified that he did not have peace of mind since the day the pastor came to see him. He was now willing to surrender his life to Jesus. Today, he is a born again believer of Jesus Christ

9. Speak What God Says

You shall not add to the word which I command you, nor take from it, that you may keep the commandments of the LORD your God which I command you.

(Deuteronomy 4:2)

"Whatever I command you, be careful to observe it; you shall not add to it nor take away from it.

(Deuteronomy 12:32)

For I testify to everyone who hears the words of the prophecy of this book: If anyone adds to these things, God will add to him the plagues that are written in this book; and if anyone takes away from the words of the book of this prophecy, God shall take away his part from the Book of Life, from the holy city, and from the things which are written in this book.

(Revelation 22:18-19)

Every word of God is pure; He is a shield to those who put their trust in Him. Do not add to His words, lest He rebuke you, and you be found a liar.

(Proverbs 30:5-6)

Honestly, we are equal in the eyes of God. The reason why many are greater than others is because of their faithfulness to God. When we speak the reality of God's Word, God will promote us in every area of our lives.

A man's gift makes room for him, and brings him before great men.
(Proverbs 18:16)

For I am not ashamed of the gospel of Christ, for it is the power of God to salvation for everyone who believes, for the Jew first and also for the Greek.
(Romans 1:16)

If you want to have a divine connection with God.

> For as the body is one and has many members, but all the members of that one body, being many, are one body, so also is Christ. For by one Spirit we were all baptized into one body—whether Jews or Greeks, whether slaves or free—and have all been made to drink into one Spirit. For in fact, the body is not one member but many. If the foot should say, "Because I am not a hand, I am not of the body," is it therefore not of the body? And if the ear should say, "Because I am not an eye, I am not of the body," is it therefore not of the body? If the whole body were an eye, where would be the hearing? If the whole were

hearing, where would be the smelling? But now God has set the members, each one of them, in the body just as He pleased. And if they were all one member, where would the body be? But now indeed there are many members, yet one body. And the eye cannot say to the hand, "I have no need of you"; nor again the head to the feet, "I have no need of you." No, much rather, those members of the body which seem to be weaker are necessary. And those members of the body which we think to be less honourable, on these we bestow greater honour; and our unpresentable parts have greater modesty, but our presentable parts have no need. But God composed the body, having given greater honour to that part which lacks it, that there should be no schism in the body, but that the members should have the same care for one another. And if one member suffers, all the members suffer with it; or if one member is honoured, all the members rejoice with it. Now you are the body of Christ, and members individually.

(1 Corinthians 12:12-27)

10. Have The Compassion of Love

Beloved, have the compassion of love in season and out of season. Do not walk by sight. We are to walk by faith. Remember what the bible says in the following Scriptures.

> Jesus said to him, "'You shall love the LORD your God with all your heart, with all your soul, and with all your mind.' This is the first and great commandment. And the second is like it: 'You shall love your neighbour as yourself.' On these two commandments hang all the Law and the Prophets."
> (Matthew 22:37-40)

> A new commandment I give to you, that you love one another; as I have loved you, that you also love one another. By this all will know that you are My disciples, if you have love for one another.
> (John 13:34-35)

> Therefore, whatever you want men to do to you, do also to them, for this is the Law and the Prophets.
> (Matthew 7:12)

> But love your enemies, do good, and lend, hoping for nothing in return; and your reward

will be great, and you will be sons of the Most High. For He is kind to the unthankful and evil.

(Luke 6:35)

Yet it shall not be so among you; but whoever desires to become great among you shall be your servant. And whoever of you desires to be first shall be slave of all. For even the Son of Man did not come to be served, but to serve, and to give His life a ransom for many.

(Mark 10:43-45)

If I then, your Lord and Teacher, have washed your feet, you also ought to wash one another's feet. For I have given you an example, that you should do as I have done to you.

(John 13:14-15)

Above all, if you want to have a divine connection with God, know that our Lord Jesus has the compassion of love. If we love Him, we should love others as Christ love also.

And Jesus, when He came out, saw a great multitude and was moved with compassion for them, because they were like sheep not having a shepherd. So He began to teach them many things.

(Mark 6:34)

"I have compassion on the multitude, because they have now continued with Me three days and have nothing to eat. And if I send them away hungry to their own houses, they will faint on the way; for some of them have come from afar."

(Mark 8:2-3)

When the Lord saw her, He had compassion on her and said to her, "Do not weep. Then He came and touched the open coffin, and those who carried him stood still. And He said, "Young man, I say to you, arise."

(Luke 7:13-14)

So, Jesus had compassion and touched their eyes. And immediately their eyes received sight, and they followed Him.

(Matthew 20:34)

For the Son of Man has come to save that which was lost. "What do you think? If a man has a hundred sheep, and one of them goes astray, does he not leave the ninety-nine and go to the mountains to seek the one that is straying? And if he should find it, assuredly, I say to you, he rejoices more over that sheep than over the ninety-nine that did not go astray.

(Matthew 18:11-13)

Truthfulness

The words of the LORD are pure words, like silver tried in a furnace of earth, purified seven times.

(Psalm 12:6)

Beloved, honestly many can be praising God and showing brotherly or sisterly love when all is well but when anything begins to inconvenience them, their true self will emerge. We know that Peter denied that he knew Jesus three times when Jesus was arrested. When he realized what he has done, Peter wept. What is the meaning of truthfulness? It is telling the truth and for one to be accurate corresponding to fact or reality.

> Now Peter sat outside in the courtyard. And a servant girl came to him, saying, "You also were with Jesus of Galilee." But he denied it before them all, saying, "I do not know what you are saying." And when he had gone out to the gateway, another girl saw him and said to those who were there, "This fellow also was with Jesus of Nazareth." But again he denied with an oath, "I do not know the Man!" And a little later those who stood by came up and said to Peter, "Surely you also are one of them, for your speech betrays you." Then he

began to curse and swear, saying, "I do not know the Man!" Immediately a rooster crowed. And Peter remembered the word of Jesus who had said to him, "Before the rooster crows, you will deny Me three times." So he went out and wept bitterly.

(Matthew 26:69-75)

When you read the book of Acts, you will see that Peter proved himself as a leader. He challenged the high priest, proving to them that Jesus is indeed the Son of God. In many occasions, even though he knew that he would lose his life, he was not afraid. Still, he proved to the enemies of God that he was the leader of the disciples of Jesus Christ. Beloved, do you know, Peter and John were ready to face the challenges that came their way.

But Peter and John answered and said to them, "Whether it is right in the sight of God to listen to you more than to God, you judge. For we cannot but speak the things which we have seen and heard."

(Acts 4:19-20)

OBEDIENCE

Now it shall come to pass, if you diligently obey the voice of the LORD your God, to observe carefully all His commandments which I command you today, that the LORD your God will set you high above all nations of the earth. And all these blessings shall come upon you and overtake you, because you obey the voice of the LORD your God: "Blessed shall you be in the city, and blessed shall you be in the country. "Blessed shall be the fruit of your body, the produce of your ground and the increase of your herds, the increase of your cattle and the offspring of your flocks. "Blessed shall be your basket and your kneading bowl. "Blessed shall you be when you come in, and blessed shall you be when you go out. "The LORD will cause your enemies who rise against you to be defeated before your face; they shall come out against you one way and flee before you seven ways."
(Deuteronomy 28:1-7)

Born again Christians, if you want to have a divine connection with God, obedient to God's word is a must. I am talking about when you are in danger or you are finding it very difficult to go on for the sake of the gospel. Still, you have to obey God.

The Scripture in 1Peter 3:13-15 says, *"And who is he who will harm you if you become followers of what is good?* But even if you should suffer for righteousness' sake, you are blessed. 'And do not be afraid of their threats, nor be troubled.' But sanctify the Lord God in your hearts, and always be ready to give a defence to everyone who asks you a reason for the hope that is in you, with meekness and fear." Above all, when Apostle Paul was arrested in Jerusalem, he continued to be obedient to God and he testified that Jesus is God.

> And when he had said this, a dissension arose between the Pharisees and the Sadducees; and the assembly was divided. For Sadducees say that there is no resurrection — and no angel or spirit; but the Pharisees confess both. Then there arose a loud outcry. And the scribes of the Pharisees' party arose and protested, saying, "We find no evil in this man; but if a spirit or an angel has spoken to him, let us not fight against God." Now when there arose a great dissension, the commander, fearing lest Paul might be pulled to pieces by them, commanded the soldiers to go down and

take him by force from among them, and bring him into the barracks. But the following night the Lord stood by him and said, "Be of good cheer, Paul; for as you have testified for Me in Jerusalem, so you must also bear witness at Rome."

(Acts 23:7-11)

But today, many would be afraid to testify about Jesus because of what they went through. Jesus appeared to Paul because of his faithfulness. Acts 23:11 says, *"But the following night the Lord stood by him and said, "Be of good cheer, Paul; for as you have testified for Me in Jerusalem, so you must also bear witness at Rome."*

NEW LIFE

Jesus answered and said to him, "Most assuredly, I say to you, unless one is born again, he cannot see the kingdom of God." Nicodemus said to Him, "How can a man be born when he is old? Can he enter a second time into his mother's womb and be born?" Jesus answered, "Most assuredly, I say to you, unless one is born of water and the Spirit, he cannot enter the kingdom of God.

(John 3:3-5)

Remember, Paul said that if anyone is in Christ, he is a new creation. Old things have passed away, behold all things have become new. Honestly, we do not go back to our former lifestyle again because Isaiah 43:18-19 says, "Do not remember the former things, nor consider the things of old. Behold, I will do a new thing, now it shall spring forth; shall you not know it? I will even make a road in the wilderness and rivers in the desert."

So, living a new life simply means repentance and to live a righteous life. Colossians 3:12-17 tells us, "Therefore, as the elect of God, holy and beloved, put on tender mercies, kindness, humility, meekness, long-suffering; bearing with one another, and forgiving one another, if anyone has a complaint against another; even as Christ forgave you, so you also must do. Above all these things put on love, which is the bond of perfection. And let the peace of God rule in your hearts, to which also you were called in one body; and be thankful. Let the word of Christ dwell in you richly in all wisdom, teaching and admonishing one another in psalms and hymns and spiritual songs, singing with grace in your hearts to the Lord. And whatever you do in word or deed, do all in the name of the Lord Jesus, giving thanks to God the Father through Him."

NEARER

Redeeming the time, because the days are evil. Therefore do not be unwise, but understand what the will of the Lord is. And do not be drunk with wine, in which is dissipation; but be filled with the Spirit, speaking to one another in psalms and hymns and spiritual songs, singing and making melody in your heart to the Lord, giving thanks always for all things to God the Father in the name of our Lord Jesus Christ.

(Ephesians 5:16-20)

Beloved, if you want to have a divine connection with God, every believer should be in church on time. We do not need to be late for Sunday service because when you are in church on time, the Angel of God will be there waiting for you, to bless you.

That is why the bible says in Mark 13:33-37, "Take heed, watch and pray; for you do not know when the time is. It is like a man going to a far country, who left his house and gave authority to his servants, and to each his work, and commanded the doorkeeper to watch. Watch therefore, for you do not know when the master of the house is coming—in the evening, at midnight, at the crowing of the rooster, or in the morning—lest, coming suddenly, he find you sleeping. And what I say to you, I say to all: Watch!"

Many are not interested to read their bible daily. They find it very difficult to read the bible. But when it is time to watch television or movies, then they will have enough strength. Even many are not interested to increase their prayer life. There are 168 hours in a week and if you set aside ten percent of that time it is about 16.8 hours. Now if you can spend at least 7 hours in a week, God will see you through.

ETERNITY

Beloved, honestly many are being carried away when they continue to commit the same sin over and over again, thinking that our Holy God will forgive us.

> Samuel also said to Saul, "The LORD sent me to anoint you king over His people, over Israel. Now therefore, heed the voice of the words of the LORD. Thus says the LORD of hosts: 'I will punish Amalek for what he did to Israel, how he ambushed him on the way when he came up from Egypt. Now go and attack Amalek, and utterly destroy all that they have,

and do not spare them. But kill both man and woman, infant and nursing child, ox and sheep, camel and donkey.'"

(1 Samuel 15:1-3)

And Saul attacked the Amalekites, from Havilah all the way to Shur, which is east of Egypt. He also took Agag king of the Amalekites alive, and utterly destroyed all the people with the edge of the sword. But Saul and the people spared Agag and the best of the sheep, the oxen, the fatlings, the lambs, and all that was good, and were unwilling to utterly destroy them. But everything despised and worthless, that they utterly destroyed. Now the word of the LORD came to Samuel, saying, "I greatly regret that I have set up Saul as king, for he has turned back from following Me, and has not performed My commandments." And it grieved Samuel, and he cried out to the LORD all night.

(1 Samuel 15:7-11)

Now the LORD sent you on a mission, and said, 'Go, and utterly destroy the sinners, the Amalekites, and fight against them until they are consumed.' Why then did you not obey the voice of the LORD? Why did you swoop down on the spoil, and do evil in the sight of the LORD?" And Saul said to Samuel, "But I have obeyed the voice of the LORD, and gone on the mission on which the LORD sent me, and brought back Agag king of Amalek; I have utterly destroyed the Amalekites. But the people took of the plunder, sheep and oxen, the best of the things which should have been utterly destroyed, to sacrifice to the LORD your God in Gilgal." So Samuel said: "Has the LORD as great delight in burnt offerings and sacrifices, as in obeying the voice of the LORD? Behold, to obey is better than sacrifice, and to heed than the fat of rams. For rebellion is as the sin of witchcraft, and stubbornness is as iniquity and idolatry. Because you have rejected the word of the LORD, He also has rejected you from being king." Then Saul said to Samuel, "I have sinned, for I have transgressed the commandment of the LORD and your words, because I feared the people and obeyed their voice. Now therefore, please pardon my sin, and return with me, that I may worship the LORD." But Samuel said to Saul, "I will not return with you, for you have rejected the word of the LORD, and the LORD has rejected you from being king over Israel." And as Samuel turned around to go away, Saul seized the edge of his robe, and it tore. So Samuel said to him, "The LORD has torn the kingdom of Israel from you today, and has given it to a neighbour of yours, who is better than you. And also the Strength of Israel will not lie nor relent. For He is not a man, that He should relent." Then he said, "I have sinned; yet honour me now, please, before the elders of my people and before Israel, and return with me, that I may worship the LORD your God." So Samuel turned back after Saul, and Saul worshiped the LORD. Then Samuel said, "Bring Agag king of the Amalekites here to me." So Agag came to him cautiously. And Agag said, "Surely the bitterness of death is past."

(1 Samuel 15:18-32)

Saul has been sinning against God, although the bible did not say so. That was why he died a shameful death. Our God is a merciful God but that does not mean that we can continue to live in sin. Look at Romans 9:15-18 which says, *"For He says to Moses, "I will have mercy on whomever I will have mercy, and I will have compassion on whomever I will have compassion." So then it is not of him who wills, nor of him who runs, but of God who shows mercy. For the Scripture says to the*

Pharaoh, "For this very purpose I have raised you up, that I may show My power in you, and that My name may be declared in all the earth." Therefore He has mercy on whom He wills, and whom He wills He hardens."

I know many who believe that when they sin repeatedly, God will forgive them. Beloved, it does not work like that.

> Then the LORD said to me, "Even if Moses and Samuel stood before Me, My mind would not be favourable toward this people. Cast them out of My sight, and let them go forth. And it shall be, if they say to you, 'Where should we go?' then you shall tell them, 'Thus says the LORD: "Such as are for death, to death; and such as are for the sword, to the sword; and such as are for the famine, to the famine; and such as are for the captivity, to the captivity."' "And I will appoint over them four forms of destruction," says the LORD: "the sword to slay, the dogs to drag, the birds of the heavens and the beasts of the earth to devour and destroy."
>
> (Jeremiah 15:1-3)

> The soul who sins shall die. The son shall not bear the guilt of the father, nor the father bear

the guilt of the son. The righteousness of the righteous shall be upon himself, and the wickedness of the wicked shall be upon himself. But if a wicked man turns from all his sins which he has committed, keeps all My statutes, and does what is lawful and right, he shall surely live; he shall not die. None of the transgressions which he has committed shall be remembered against him; because of the righteousness which he has done, he shall live.

(Ezekiel 18:20-22)

CO-OPERATE

Now all who believed were together, and had all things in common, and sold their possessions and goods, and divided them among all, as anyone had need. So continuing daily with one accord in the temple, and breaking bread from house to house, they ate their food with gladness and simplicity of heart, praising God and having favour with all the people. And the Lord added to the church daily those who were being saved.

(Acts 2:44-47)

We need to be in unity as believers of Jesus Christ because, in those days, the apostles were taking things in common. If we should do this same thing, honestly, God will be happy with us.

Now the multitude of those who believed were of one heart and one soul; neither did anyone say that any of the things he possessed was his own, but they had all things in common.
(Acts 4:32)

Beloved, if you want to have a divine connection with God, in church, we must be in unity, in business we must be in unity. In Agape Love, in giving, in ministry, in helping one another, in sincerity and honesty, we must be in unity.

Ladies and gentlemen, this is the time we should begin to ask others about their various problems. We do not have to wait for them to come to us. Rather, we should help them immediately. So, God will be happy with us.

Be diligent to know the state of your flocks, and attend to your herds.
(Proverbs 27:23)

TESTIFY

The righteousness of Your testimonies is everlasting; Give me understanding, and I shall live. I cry out with my whole heart; hear me, O LORD! I will keep Your statutes. I cry out to You; Save me, and I will keep Your testimonies.
(Psalm 119:144-146)

Today, many are afraid to testify the goodness of God in their lives. Honestly, testimony is the sharing of God's deeds in our lives. When we begin to experience it, God will make a way when there seems to be no way.

Paul was the one God used to shame the devil after the death of Stephen so that the word of God would continue to this day. God told Saul, who later became Paul that he would suffer many things for His name. Although Apostle Paul was instructed not to go to Jerusalem when the prophecy was given to him, still he went. God appeared to make him stronger as I have mentioned earlier. When Apostle Paul was defending himself before King Agrippa, he testified how God had arrested him when he was on his way to Damascus.

They knew me from the first, if they were willing to testify, that according to the strictest sect of our religion I lived a Pharisee.

(Acts 26:5)

Paul was telling King Agrippa that the accusers knew him too well as the former persecutor of the people of God. If you read Acts 26 you will read how he testified the kind of life he used to live. Apostle Paul also testified about Jesus. As he was testifying about Jesus to the king, he asked the king in Acts 26:27-28, *"King Agrippa, do you believe in the prophet? I know that you do believe."* Then *Agrippa said to Paul, 'You almost persuade me to become a Christian.'"*

Beloved, if you want to have a divine connection with God, we have seen how King Agrippa confessed to Paul that he nearly persuaded him to become a Christian. Nobody knows whether he became a Christian or not for the bible did not tell us. If we can preach to people and they say the same thing as what King Agrippa did, we can leave the rest to God. 1 Corinthians 3:7 tells us that it is neither he who plants nor he who waters is anything, but only God who makes the increase. Moreover, God would be happy with us because it is not by might nor by power but by the power of the

Holy Spirit. Take note to speak to the people in the government also.

IMITATE

Beloved, we should not be afraid to vindicate the gospel because God is real. We should be imitators of the Word that is written in the bible.

That you do not become sluggish, but imitate those who through faith and patience inherit the promises.
(Hebrews 6:12)

Today, many are presenting themselves bearing good names but when it is time to preach the gospel, they will not be interested. Ladies and gentlemen, what do you think about it? Many believe that it is enough to live a righteous life without making any effort of preaching the gospel to others with boldness. At times, I do not feel comfortable when I see many Christians are not proving themselves as believers of Christ. When you ask some Christians whether they are Christians, they would be afraid to give you an honest answer. But the bible says in 1Corinthians 9:23, *"Now this I do for the gospel's sake, that I may be partaker of it with you."*

ORIGINAL

Beloved, we are originals before the Almighty God. Do not see yourself as an imitation before God. Rather, see yourself as an original whom God has called to be His own through Jesus Christ our Lord. Know that there is no partiality with God for He is not the author of confusion but of peace and all things work together for good to them that love God.

"But you are a chosen generation, a royal priesthood, a holy nation, His own special people, that you may proclaim the praises of Him who called you out of darkness into His marvellous light. Who once were not a people but are now the people of God, who had not obtained mercy but now have obtained mercy."

(1 Peter 2:9-10)

Remember that the stone the builders have rejected has become the chief cornerstone. When the Lord is on our side, what can man do to us? It is the Lord's doing. We should rejoice and be glad in it. We should give thanks to God always because it is not by might nor by power nor by our kindness that brings us to repentance. We should know that we are originals in God's sight because we have a focus and our focus is to make it to heaven where everything in heaven is covered with gold and precious jewels. It is better to put our trust in the Lord than to put confidence in man. Nowadays, many believers do not know who they really are in Christ Jesus, because of one thing or another. We need to know that it is our faith as originals in Christ that would make God to open the gates of righteousness in us and the gate of righteousness is the gate of the Lord, which the righteous shall enter. Blessed is he who comes in the name of the Lord. It is the greatest miracle for those who come in the name of the Lord. If you want to have a divine connection with God when we discover that we are originals in the sight of God, we should face and overcome any challenges that come along our way.

Blessed is the man who walks not in the counsel of the ungodly, nor stands in the path of sinners, nor sits in the seat of the scornful. But his delight is in the law of the Lord and in His law he meditates day and night. He shall be like a tree planted by the rivers of water that brings forth its fruits in its season whose leaf also shall not wither and whatever he does shall prosper.

(Psalm 1:1-3)

Nowadays, many Christians would like to bow down to non-believers because of the riches of this world. To God be the glory, Mordecai did not bow down to Haman. We need to know as a Christian, that our God is able to lift us up according to His own timing. In addition, we should know that once we have become the originals before God, temptations will come in every area of our life to subdue us, but if God is on our side, who can be against us.

And we know that all things work together for good to those who love God, to those who are the called according to His purpose.
(Romans 8:28)

NARROW GATE

Beloved, what is the actual meaning of the Narrow Gate? Jesus said in Matthew 7:13-14, "Enter by the narrow gate; for wide is the gate and broad is the way that leads to destruction, and there are many who go in by it. Because narrow is the gate and difficult is the way which leads to life, and there are few who find it."

The word Narrow Gate simply means a way or a life that is pleasing to God. It is also the way to make it to heaven and to overcome every obstacle that may bring shame to our Christian life. Remember that the bible says in Isaiah 53:5, "But He was wounded for our transgressions, He was bruised for our iniquities; the chastisement for our peace was upon Him, and by His stripes we are healed."

> Therefore God also has highly exalted Him and given Him the name which is above every name, that at the name of Jesus every knee should bow, of those in heaven, and of those on earth, and of those under the earth, and that every tongue should confess that Jesus Christ is Lord, to the glory of God the Father. Therefore, my beloved, as you have always obeyed, not as in my presence only, but now much more in my absence, work out your own salvation with fear and trembling; for it is God who works in you both to will and to do for His good pleasure. Do all things without complaining and disputing, that you may become blameless and harmless, children of God without fault in the midst of a crooked and perverse generation, among whom you shine as lights in the world, holding fast the word of life, so that I may rejoice in the day of Christ that I have not run in vain or laboured in vain.
>
> (Philippians 2:9-16)

Honestly, narrow gate leads to heaven because God has taken me there and I saw people walking through the gate and I followed them. Beloved, when you passed God's test, entering the narrow gate is your portion. Jesus is the narrow gate. So, put your faith in Jesus and it shall be well with you. Entering the Narrow Gate signifies the heart's acceptance of Christ's holy teaching. Walking through the Narrow Way means to have a steady perseverance in faith and obedience to the Lord Jesus, to overcome all opposition, to reject every temptation of forsaking the path of loyalty to Him and shutting out all self-pleasing and self-seeking in our lives.

There are two types of gates:

- The Worldly Gate - (Wide Gate)
- The Heavenly Gate - (Narrow Gate)

The Worldly Gate (Wide Gate)

The bible tells us that wide is the gate and broad is the way that leads to destruction, and there are many who go in by it. Why is it that many are entering the wide gate? Many are living in sin that will only lead them to hell fire. When someone joined a secret cult or someone sowed his life to the devil, he is setting himself for destruction.

He who sows iniquity will reap sorrow, and the rod of his anger will fail.
(Proverbs 22:8)

So if you are living in the flesh, be it known to you that anything can happen to you. That is why many are dying prematurely when they are not meant to die yet.

Enter by the narrow gate; for wide is the gate and broad is the way that leads to destruction, and there are many who go in by it.
(Matthew 7:13)

There are even many who know what it takes to make it to heaven but because of their selfishness, they will continue to live in sin over and over again.

The soul who sins shall die. The son shall not bear the guilt of the father, nor the father bear the guilt of the son. The righteousness of the righteous shall be upon himself, and the wickedness of the wicked shall be upon himself.
(Ezekiel 18:20)

So, anything we do apart from the will of God is eternal destruction. It is a battle of someone living in the flesh fighting against each other. For example, the bible tells us that the people of Israel were fighting against themselves because of the idol worshippers.

> Now when Moses saw that the people were unrestrained for Aaron had not restrained them, to their shame among their enemies, then Moses stood in the entrance of the camp, and said, "Whoever is on the LORD's side come to me!" And all the sons of Levi gathered themselves together to him. And he said to them, "Thus says the LORD God of Israel: 'Let every man put his sword on his side, and go in and out from entrance to entrance throughout the camp, and let every man kill his brother, every man his companion, and every man his neighbour.'" So the sons of Levi did according to the word of Moses. And about three thousand men of the people fell that day.
>
> (Exodus 32:25-28)

Beloved, if you want to have a divine connection with God, if you are not on the Lord's side, then you are walking through the wide gate. We have seen that when Moses went to the mountain, some of the people of Israel were restless and began to rebel against God.

> Now when the people saw that Moses delayed coming down from the mountain, the people gathered together to Aaron, and said to him, "Come, make us gods that shall go before us; for as for this Moses, the man who brought us up out of the land of Egypt, we do not know what has become of him." And Aaron said to them, "Break off the golden earrings which are in the ears of your wives, your sons, and your daughters, and bring them to me." So all the people broke off the golden earrings which were in their ears, and brought them to Aaron. And he received the gold from their hand, and he fashioned it with an engraving tool, and made a melded calf. Then they said, "This is your god, O Israel, that brought you out of the land of Egypt!" So when Aaron saw it, he built an altar before it. And Aaron made a proclamation and said, "Tomorrow is a feast to the LORD."
>
> (Exodus 32:1-5)

And Moses said to Aaron, "What did this people do to you that you have brought so great a sin upon them?" So Aaron said, "Do not let the anger of my lord become hot. You know the people, that they are set on evil. For they said to me, 'Make us gods that shall go before us; as for this Moses, the man who brought us out of the land of Egypt, we do not know what has become of him.' And I said to them, 'Whoever has any gold, let them break it off.' So they gave it to me, and I cast it into the fire, and this calf came out."

(Exodus 32:21-24)

These were the people God brought out of the wilderness. Yet, because of their selfishness, they decided to worship idols. They were restless and insecure. So, when Moses delayed in coming down from the mountain they decided to make for themselves an idol which they could worship, forgetting everything that God has done for them. Moses should not be blamed for being on the mountain for so long because he was up in the mountain as instructed by God, not for himself but for the people of Israel. When Moses saw that the people were running wild because Aaron did not restrain them he stood at the entrance of the camp and said to the people, "Whoever is on the LORD's side, come to me." And all the sons of Levi gathered themselves together to him.

And he said to them, "Thus says the LORD God of Israel: 'Let every man put his sword on his side, and go in and out from entrance to entrance throughout the camp, and let every man kill his brother, every man his companion, and every man his neighbour.'" So the sons of Levi did according to the word of Moses. And about three thousand men of the people fell that day.

(Exodus 32:27-28)

Therefore, we have seen what happened to the people of Israel who rebelled against God. According to the Scripture in Jeremiah 10:6-10 it says, "Inasmuch as there is none like You, O LORD You are great, and Your name is great in might, who would not fear You, O King of the nations? For this is Your rightful due. For among all the wise men of the nations, and in all their kingdoms, there is none like You. But they are altogether dull-hearted and foolish; a wooden idol is a worthless doctrine. Silver is beaten into plates; it is brought from Tarshish, and gold from Uphaz, the work of the craftsman and of the hands of the metalsmith; blue and purple are their clothing; they are all the work of skillful men. But the LORD is the true God; He is the living God and the everlasting King. At His wrath the earth will tremble, and the nations will not be able to endure His indignation."

The Heavenly Gate (Narrow Gate)

Jesus is The Way, The Truth and The Life. Nobody goes to the Father except through Jesus Christ. The heavenly gate is real and is not a fake. Many in the bible went through tremendous trials and temptation but they continued to be steadfast in Christ and made it to heaven.

God will enable us to have the ability to go through trials and temptations and turn our weaknesses into strengths as we pass through the heavenly narrow gate. Apostle Peter said in 1 Peter 4:12-19, "Beloved, do not think it strange concerning the fiery trial which is to try you, as though some strange thing happened to you; but rejoice to the extent that you partake of Christ's sufferings, that when His glory is revealed, you may also be glad with exceeding joy. If you are reproached for the name of Christ, blessed are you, for the Spirit of glory and of God rests upon you. On their part He is blasphemed, but on your part He is glorified. But let none of you suffer as a murderer, a thief, an evildoer, or as a busybody in other people's matters. Yet if anyone suffers as a Christian, let him not be ashamed, but let him glorify God in this matter. For the time has come for judgment to begin at the house of God; and if it begins with us first, what will be the end of those who do not obey the gospel of God? Now "If the righteous one is scarcely saved, where will the ungodly and the sinner appear?" Therefore let those who suffer according to the will of God commit their souls to Him in doing good, as to a faithful Creator."

Entering a narrow gate is also like when we are doing good in the eyes of God but in the eyes of men, it would seem like we are doing bad. Nevertheless, we continue to be steadfast and trust God. It is also living a righteous life.

Shall We Pray

Forever O LORD, I thank You for the word I have read in this chapter and I decree that starting from this hour onward my life will never remain the same again. I claim every word that I have read in this chapter. Let it be my portion.

Your word says in Psalm 125:1-5, "Those who trust in the LORD are like Mount Zion, which cannot be moved, but abides forever. As the mountains surround Jerusalem, so the LORD surrounds His people from this time forth and forever. For the sceptre of wickedness shall not rest on the land allotted to the righteous, lest the righteous reach out their hands to iniquity. Do good, O LORD, to those who are good, and to those who are upright in their hearts. As for such as turn aside to their crooked ways, the LORD shall lead them away with the workers of iniquity. Peace be upon Israel!" O LORD let Your grace be sufficient upon me so that your divine connection will be my portion in every area of my life.

In Jesus mighty name. Amen.

CHAPTER 2

DOUBLE PORTION ANOINTING

❧

And so it was, when they had crossed over, that Elijah said to Elisha, "Ask! What may I do for you, before I am taken away from you?" Elisha said, "Please let a double portion of your spirit be upon me."
(2 Kings 2:9)

Beloved, it is not by might or by power but by the power of the Holy Spirit for one to receive a double portion of anointing. Elisha to receive a double portion of anointing from Elijah it is because he was faithful.

Now when the sons of the prophets who were from Jericho saw him, they said, "The spirit of Elijah rests on Elisha." And they came to meet him, and bowed to the ground before him.
(2 Kings 2:15)

We have seen that Elijah told Elisha to ask what he could do for him. Elisha did not ask for one million dollars or to live forever. Rather, Elisha asked for a double portion of Elijah's anointing.

Beloved, what do you understand about Elisha's request? According to my view, Elisha has a focus and his focus is to set as many captives free because he wants to make it to heaven, His intention is not the earthly things. Rather, he has a purpose and his purpose came to pass.

I hope we can learn from Elisha's attitude towards Elijah and know what we need to do. But today, many will be carried away with the things of the world. Honestly, there are many believers in this end time who would be in the position of Elisha. Instead of asking for a double portion of anointing, they would rather ask for wealth.

> Do not love the world or the things in the world. If anyone loves the world, the love of the Father is not in him. For all that is in the world—the lust of the flesh, the lust of the eyes, and the pride of life—is not of the Father but is of the world. And the world is passing away, and the lust of it; but he who does the will of God abides forever. Little children, it is the last hour; and as you have heard that the Antichrist is coming, even

now many antichrists have come, by which we know that it is the last hour.

(1 John 2:15-18)

But those who desire to be rich fall into temptation and a snare, and into many foolish and harmful lusts which drown men in destruction and perdition. For the love of money is a root of all kinds of evil, for which some have strayed from the faith in their greediness, and pierced themselves through with many sorrows. But you, O man of God, flee these things and pursue righteousness, godliness, faith, love, patience, gentleness.

(1 Timothy 6:9-11)

We have seen that the love of money is the root of all evil. Beloved, the Lord's eyes are not closed or His ears are not heavy, neither is His hand shortened. Rather, it is because of our selfishness, we are not able to receive His blessing.

Behold, if you want to have a divine connection from God, the LORD's hand is not shortened, that it cannot save; nor His ear heavy, that it cannot hear. But your iniquities have separated you from your God; and your sins have hidden His face from you, so that He will not hear.

(Isaiah 59:1-2)

Remember, King Solomon asked God for wisdom and God not only blessed him with wisdom but God also blessed him with riches and honour.

At Gibeon the LORD appeared to Solomon in a dream by night; and God said, "Ask! What shall I give you?" And Solomon said: "You have shown great mercy to Your servant David my father, because he walked before You in truth, in righteousness, and in uprightness of heart with You; You have continued this great kindness for him, and You have given him a son to sit on his throne, as it is this day. Now, O LORD my God, You have made Your servant king instead of my father David, but I am a little child; I do not know how to go out or come in. And Your servant is in the midst of Your people whom You have chosen, a great people, too numerous to be numbered or counted. Therefore give to Your servant an understanding heart to judge Your people, that I may discern between good and evil. For who is able to judge this great people of Yours?" The speech pleased the Lord, that Solomon had asked this thing. Then God said to him: "Because you have asked this thing, and have not asked long life for yourself, nor have asked riches for yourself, nor have asked the life of your enemies, but have asked for yourself understanding to discern justice, behold, I have done according to your words; see, I have given you a wise and understanding heart, so that there has not been anyone like you before you, nor shall any like you arise after you. And I have also given you what you have not asked: both riches and honour, so that there shall not be anyone like you among the kings all your days. So if you walk in My ways, to keep My statutes and My commandments, as your father David walked, then I will lengthen your days."

(1 Kings 3:5-14)

We have seen how God blessed King Solomon because he did not ask anything for his own benefit but asked for wisdom so that he would be given wisdom that he may know how to discern between what was good and evil when he judge God's people. God who searched the heart knew that King Solomon was sincere when he asked for wisdom and God blessed him with more than he asked for. If you want to have a divine connection from God, I believe that we should ask God to direct our paths so that we may know the area He is calling us instead of demanding from God to supply our needs. As God has blessed King Solomon more than what he has requested, God will also do it for us, in Jesus mighty name.

The counsel of the LORD stands forever, the plans of His heart to all generations. Blessed is the nation whose God is the LORD, the people He has chosen as His own inheritance. The LORD looks from heaven; He sees all the sons of men. From the place of His dwelling He looks on all the inhabitants of the earth; He fashions their hearts individually; He considers all their works.

Psalm 33:11-15

We have seen that the eyes of God are upon His people so we do not need to worry about what to put on or what to eat because Jesus said in Matthew 6:24-26, *""No one can serve two masters; for either he will hate the one and love the other, or else he will be loyal to the one and despise the other. You cannot serve God and mammon. "Therefore I say to you, do not worry about your life, what you will eat or what you will drink; nor about your body, what you will put on. Is not life more than food and the body more than clothing? Look at the birds of the air, for they neither sow nor reap nor gather into barns; yet your heavenly Father feeds them. Are you not of more value than they?"*

Beloved, let us not deceive ourselves because God is not mocked. Whatever we sow we shall reap. When we obey Him, whatever it takes to prosper, God will show us how it will be done. There are various type of double portion anointing. When we give God something tangible, He will give us more than what we have given to Him. Remember, no man or woman can out give God.

No wonder the bible says in 2 Corinthians 9:6-10, "But this I say: He who sows sparingly will also reap sparingly, and he who sows bountifully will also reap bountifully. So let each one give as he purposes in his heart, not grudgingly or of necessity; for God loves a cheerful giver. And God is able to make all grace abound toward you, that you, always having all sufficiency in all things, may have an abundance for every good work. As it is written: "He has dispersed abroad, He has given to the poor; His righteousness endures forever." Now may He who supplies seed to the sower, and bread for food, supply and multiply the seed you have sown and increase the fruits of your righteousness"

Double Portion Anointing Can Make One To Live A Long Life

I know of a preacher from American who has been preaching for 67 years. Even though he was 83 years old, he was still very strong and active whenever he preaches. Do you know that this preacher can stand up and preach for four hours?

Those who trust in the LORD are like Mount Zion, which cannot be moved, but abides forever. As the mountains surround Jerusalem, so the LORD surrounds His people from this time forth and forever.

(Psalm 125:1-2)

Double Portion Anointing Can Be Transformed By The Anointing Oil

Then Samuel took the horn of oil and anointed him in the midst of his brothers; and the Spirit of the LORD came upon David from that day forward. So Samuel arose and went to Ramah.

1 Samuel 16:13

We have seen that David was anointed by Samuel and because of the anointing he received, he was able to defeat Goliath and later became the king of Judah. 2 Samuel 5:1-5 says, "Then all the tribes of Israel came to David at Hebron and spoke, saying, "Indeed we are your bone and your flesh. Also, in time past, when Saul was king over us, you were the one who led Israel out and brought them in; and the LORD said to you, 'You shall shepherd My people Israel, and be ruler over Israel.'" Therefore all the elders of Israel came to the king at Hebron, and King David made a covenant with them at Hebron before the LORD. And they anointed David king over Israel. David was thirty years old when he began to reign, and he reigned forty years. In Hebron he reigned over Judah seven years and six months, and in Jerusalem he reigned thirty-three years over all Israel and Judah."

Do you know why David was able to defeat Goliath and became the king of Israel? It is because of his faithfulness to God. Remember that God does not look at people's appearance.

> So Saul clothed David with his Armor, and he put a bronze helmet on his head; he also clothed him with a coat of mail. David fastened his sword to his Armor and tried to walk, for he

had not tested them. And David said to Saul, "I cannot walk with these, for I have not tested them." So David took them off. Then he took his staff in his hand; and he chose for himself five smooth stones from the brook, and put them in a shepherd's bag, in a pouch which he had, and his sling was in his hand. And he drew near to the Philistine. So the Philistine came, and began drawing near to David, and the man who bore the shield went before him. And when the Philistine looked about and saw David, he disdained him; for he was only a youth, ruddy and good-looking. So the Philistine said to David, "Am I a dog, that you come to me with sticks?" And the Philistine cursed David by his gods. And the Philistine said to David, "Come to me, and I will give your flesh to the birds of the air and the beasts of the field!" Then David said to the Philistine, "You come to me with a sword, with a spear, and with a javelin. But I come to you in the name of the LORD of hosts, the God of the armies of Israel, whom you have defied. This day the LORD will deliver you into my hand, and I will strike you and take your head from you. And this day I will give the carcasses of the camp of the Philistines to the birds of the air and the wild beasts of the earth, that all the earth may know that there is a God in Israel. Then all this assembly shall know that the LORD does not save with sword and spear; for the battle is the LORD's, and He will give you into our hands." So it was, when the Philistine arose and came and drew near to meet David, that David hurried and ran toward the army to meet the Philistine. Then David put his hand in his bag and took out a stone; and he slung it and struck the Philistine in his forehead, so that the stone sank into his forehead, and he fell on his face to the earth. So David prevailed over the Philistine with a sling and a stone, and struck the Philistine and killed him. But there was no sword in the hand of David. Therefore David ran and stood over the Philistine, took his sword and drew it out of its sheath and killed him, and cut off his head with it. And when the Philistines saw that their champion was dead, they fled. Now the men of Israel and Judah arose and shouted, and pursued the Philistines as far as the entrance of the valley and to the gates of Ekron. And the wounded of the Philistines fell along the road to Shaaraim, even as far as Gath and Ekron.

(1 Samuel 17:38-52)

1 Samuel 17:40 says, "Then he took his staff in his hand; and he chose for himself five smooth stones from the brook, and put them in a shepherd's bag, in a pouch which he had, and his sling was in his hand. And he drew near to the Philistine." Do you know that the five stones David used to kill Goliath represent JESUS? More so, David proved to the people of Israel that they are serving the Living God. What do you think will happen if Goliath were to defeat the people of Israel with his challenges? Remember that if Goliath were to defeat David, today it will be recorded in the history. The battle between David and Goliath was a battle between God and Satan. So, we need to make use of our faith when we are anointed by God. Do you know because of our faithfulness God can still increase our anointing to become a double portion anointing?

When we are anointed by God, we do not have to be afraid of the devil. Rather, we should exercise our faith through Christ who strengthens us. David is ready to lose his life in the battle between him and Goliath. Beloved, are you ready to face challenges when they come your way, when you have a double portion of anointing from God?

Shall We Pray

Forever O Lord your Word is infallible and indestructible. We love You O Lord because Your loving kindness endures forever. We give you all the praise and adoration. May Your name be highly lifted up, in the name of Jesus Christ.

We ask You to forgive us and we ask You to give us the grace to overcome sin because the bible says in Romans 6:23, *"For the wages of sin is death, but the gift of God is eternal life in Christ Jesus our Lord."*

We thank You for forgiving us our iniquities done knowingly or unknowingly, in the mighty name of Jesus Christ.

O Lord we ask You to transfer the double portion of anointing from Elijah to Elisha upon us. According to 2 Kings 2:9 says, "And so it was, when they had crossed over, that Elijah said to Elisha, "Ask! What may I do for you, before I am taken away from you?" Elisha said, "Please let a double portion of your spirit be upon me.""

We ask You O LORD, to used me to defeat every Goliath in my life as You did with David.

Blessed be Your Holy Name. In the name of Jesus. Amen.

CHAPTER 3

DO YOUR PART IN GOD'S WORK

※

Mary Magdalene was the first person who saw Jesus after His resurrection.

> But Mary stood outside by the tomb weeping, and as she wept she stooped down and looked into the tomb. And she saw two angels in white sitting, one at the head and the other at the feet, where the body of Jesus had lain. Then they said to her, "Woman, why are you weeping?" She said to them, "Because they have taken away my Lord, and I do not know where they have laid Him." Now when she had said this, she turned around and saw Jesus standing there, and did not know that it was Jesus. Jesus said to her, "Woman, why are you weeping? Whom are you seeking?" She,

supposing Him to be the gardener, said to Him, "Sir, if You have carried Him away, tell me where You have laid Him, and I will take Him away." Jesus said to her, "Mary!" She turned and said to Him, "Rabboni!" (which is to say, Teacher). Jesus said to her, "Do not cling to Me, for I have not yet ascended to My Father; but go to My brethren and say to them, 'I am ascending to My Father and your Father, and to My God and your God.'" Mary Magdalene came and told the disciples that she had seen the Lord, and that He had spoken these things to her. Then, the same day at evening, being the first day of the week, when the doors were shut where the disciples were assembled, for fear of the Jews, Jesus came and stood in the midst, and said to them, "Peace be with you."

(John 20:11-19)

Beloved, we have seen that Mary Magdalene was the first who met Jesus at the tomb. Can you imagine, Mary Magdalene was not one of Jesus twelve disciples. The bible tells us that she was among those who were supporting the ministry of Jesus Christ.

Now it came to pass, afterward, that He went through every city and village, preaching and bringing the glad tidings of the kingdom of God. And the twelve were with Him, and certain women who had been healed of evil spirits and infirmities—Mary called Magdalene, out of whom had come seven demons and Joanna the wife of Chuza, Herod's steward, and Susanna, and many others who provided for Him from their substance.

(Luke 8:1-3)

Surprisingly, Mary Magdalene did not deny our Lord Jesus as the other disciples did, as mentioned in Mathew. Rather, she was already at the tomb on the morning of the third day even though she knew she would be risking her life by going down to the tomb. Nevertheless, she was the first to see Jesus after His resurrection.

Jesus said to her, "Mary!" She turned and said to Him, "Rabboni!" (which is to say, Teacher). Jesus said to her, "Do not cling to Me, for I have not yet ascended to My Father; but go to My brethren and say to them, 'I am ascending to My Father and your Father, and to My God and your God.'"

(John 20:16-17)

Beloved, can you believe it. It was Mary Magdalene who was sent by our Lord to tell the disciples that she has seen the Lord and that He has risen from the dead. Why was she the first to meet Jesus at the tomb? It was because she was not afraid and she was ready to die for Christ. She truly believed that Jesus would resurrect on the third day. Peter, who received the revelation of who Jesus was.

Simon Peter answered and said, "You are the Christ, the Son of the living God."
(Matthew 16:16)

Still, he denied Jesus three times after Jesus was arrested. Beloved, do you know it was very shameful when we know everything that we need to do to make it to heaven but when afflictions and tribulations come our way, at times we will not behave as a mature Christian. Remember that if Mary Magdalene did not risk her life by going to the tomb of Jesus, do you think that she would be the first to have seen Jesus after His resurrection?

And you will be hated by all for My name's sake. But he who endures to the end will be saved.
(Matthew 10:22)

We should learn to endure in every area of our lives because nobody knows when the hour shall come.

Ladies and gentlemen, if you want to have a divine connection from God, do you know that it is not by might nor by power for Mary Magdalene to be the first to see Jesus when He was resurrected from the tomb? There is another man who did something spectacular. His name was Joseph of Arimathea. He did something that has made many to believe that Jesus actually died and rose again on the third day.

But now Christ is risen from the dead, and has become the firstfruits of those who have fallen asleep. For since by man came death, by Man also came the resurrection of the dead.

(1 Corinthians 15:20-21)

Now when evening has come there came a rich man from Arimathea named Joseph who himself had also become a disciple of Jesus. This man sent to Pilate and asked for the body of Jesus. Then Pilate commanded that the body be given to him. When Joseph had taken the body, he wrapped it in clean linen cloth. And laid it in his new tomb which he had hewn out of the rock and he rolled a large stone against the door of the tomb, and departed."

(Matthew 27:58-60)

Joseph of Arimathea was one of the greatest heroes mentioned in the bible. It seems that his heroism in human history is mainly unrecognized. He played a significant role in the history of mankind and I believe we will come to understand how important it is for us to play every role our God has set before us. Joseph of Arimathea is not mentioned anywhere else in the bible accept in the Gospel on the accounts of Jesus burial.

Scripture tells us that Joseph of Arimathea was a good and a just man. He was also a rich man and a prominent council member. He had also become a disciple of Jesus Christ. After they have crucified Jesus, Joseph of Arimathea took courage and went secretly to Pilate and asked for the body of Jesus even though this would mean endangering himself. Joseph of Arimathea, being a prominent council member gave him access to come before Pilate. Mark 15:43.

There were others who believed that Jesus was the Messiah, but were confused by His death. Joseph's conviction, courage and commitment to Jesus and to the truth led him to stand in the gap when God revealed to him to do so.

What he did made possible the striking witness of the empty tomb, which caused many to believe in the resurrection of the Son of God.

> And if Christ is not risen, then our preaching is empty and your faith is also empty. Yes, and we are found false witnesses of God, because we have testified of God that He raised up Christ, whom He did not raise up—if in fact the dead do not rise. For if the dead do not rise, then Christ is not risen. And if Christ is not risen, your faith is futile; you are still in your sins! Then also those who have fallen asleep in Christ have perished. If in this life only we have hope in Christ, we are of all men the most pitiable.
> (1 Corinthians 15:14-19)

Beloved, do you know that this man played one of the greatest roles in the scripture. What a testimony to show how much he loved Jesus and how focused he was on seeing the truth of God's Word come to pass, even though this would mean that he would not be able to take part in the Passover celebration. Perhaps he recognized that Jesus was the Passover Lamb.

Jesus said in Mathew 10:37-38, "He who loves father or mother more than Me is not worthy of Me.

And he who loves son or daughter more than Me is not worthy of Me. And he who does not take his cross and follow after Me is not worthy of Me."

Beloved, whatever role God has called you to play in this world, especially in your ministry, do it in obedience to Him. It does not matter whether you are being exposed or not, for the eyes of God is on you. Many pastors in some countries I have been to, wanted me to walk with them and they are willing to pay any amount of money for me to walk with them. But God has not called me to do that. Paul said *"Not of him who wills, nor of him who runs but of God who shows mercy."* If God has called you to hold a position, do it willingly.

Last year my wife and I wanted to go to Japan for a holiday. We have bought our air tickets and gotten my Japanese visa. But God spoke to me that we should not go to Japan but we should go to India instead to set the captives free. By His grace we were able to get our tickets to India at the last minutes and went there as the Lord has instructed us. There were a lot of testimonies received when during our visit to India. There was a woman who wanted to commit suicide because she has been suffering from a liver problem.

As I was preaching, the Lord revealed to me about her problem and that she did not have any hope of living. I prayed for her and by the special grace of God, her problem went away. The following day she went to see the doctor and the doctor told her that she has totally recovered. There was no longer any problem with her liver. I realized then why God wanted me to go to India. Not only in that place; I went to many cities in India and God really used me to set the captives free from their problems.

Beloved, if you want to have a divine connection from God listen what the word of God says in Luke 4:18, "The Spirit of God is upon me because He has anointed me to preach the gospel to the poor, He has sent me to heal the broken hearted, to proclaim liberty to the captives, and recovery of sight to the blind, to set at liberty those who are oppressed to proclaim the acceptable year of the Lord."

Some time ago, I went on a journey to Libya by faith. It took me six weeks to reach Libya through the desert. Libya is a non-Christian country. Any church you find will be underground except for the Anglican and Catholic churches. It is very risky to preach in Libya. When I was there I happened to meet a man of God. I told him who I was and that I came to Libya by faith and to preach the gospel. He told me to bring my bag so that he could keep it for me. He gave me an apartment to stay where the ministers of the gospel stayed. He announced to them that I was in charge of that place. Honestly speaking, I did not know anyone in Libya but by the special grace of God, I met this man. During that time I was doing a one year fasting. While I was there I continued my fasting but on Sunday I would attend church service. When I was at the church I discovered that there were many pastors there and that they were competing to have the opportunity to preach.

That he that competes in athletics will not be crowned unless he competes according to the rules.

(2 Timothy 2:5)

Then God spoke to me that I would visit all the cities in Libya to proclaim His gospel of salvation. God showed to me again what was going on in Libya, like prostitution and fraud. I discovered all these abominations were done by foreigners in that country. When I went from city to city I discovered some of the foreigners were using their wives or girlfriends for prostitution. I have to share the gospel to them. Honestly speaking I visited almost all the cities in Libya to set the captives free and I plant churches in some of the cities and later handed them over to the pastors. While I was in Libya for six months, the Lord spoke to me to go to Egypt because many people are lost spiritually.

"My people are destroyed for lack of knowledge."
(Hosea 4:6)

It was not easy for a black man to go from Libya to Egypt by road because Libya has a common boundary with Egypt. I asked God how I could go to Egypt. Then God began to reveal to me that I should go there by road. The city where I was residing, was about seven to eight hours from the border. Before this, I had asked my countrymen whether it was possible to cross over to Egypt by road but they told me before it was possible but it has now become very difficult to do so. But by the special grace of God, I was able to reach Egypt. I went to Egypt not knowing anybody. To God be the glory I visited most of the cities setting the captives free. I was in Egypt for five months.

If you preach the gospel willingly you will have a reward.
(1 Corinthian 9:17)

CHAPTER 4

JESUS AND THE SAMARITAN WOMAN

☙❧

The story between Jesus and the Samaritan woman was a divine connection by God.

> But He needed to go through Samaria. So He came to a city of Samaria which is called Sychar, near the plot of ground that Jacob gave to his son Joseph. Now Jacob's well was there. Jesus therefore, being wearied from His journey, sat thus by the well. It was about the sixth hour. A woman of Samaria came to draw water. Jesus said to her, "Give Me a drink." *For His disciples had gone away into the city to buy food.*
>
> (John 4:4-8)

We have seen that the disciples of Jesus have gone to buy some food. If they had not gone to buy some food, the Samaritan woman would probably not have the courage to speak with Jesus openly. Also, the disciples would probably distract Jesus from interacting with the Samaritan woman. I hope you understand what I am saying. I also believe that our Lord Jesus knew the exact time the Samaritan woman would be coming to the well to draw some water. That was why He was there at that specific time.

Jesus said to her, "Go, call your husband, and come here." The woman answered and said, "I have no husband." Jesus said to her, "You have well said, 'I have no husband,' for you have had five husbands, and the one whom you now have is not your husband; in that you spoke truly."

(John 4:16-18)

We have seen that she has had five husbands and was dating another man. Beloved, we should not lose hope in whatever circumstances we may be in. Even though you may have a bad reputation right now, that does not matter. Do not give up so easily. This is the time to turn your weaknesses into strength. I hope you understand what I am saying. This Samaritan woman could have been praying for years for a breakthrough but because of her bad reputation, no decent person would want to be associated with her. But at the appointed time, she met Jesus and proved her calling that God has bestowed upon her.

And many of the Samaritans of that city believed in Him because of the word of the woman who testified, "He told me all that I ever did."

(John 4:39)

ZACCHAEUS AND JESUS

Then Jesus entered and passed through Jericho. Now behold, there was a man named Zacchaeus who was a chief tax collector, and he was rich. And he sought to see who Jesus was, but could not because of the crowd, for he was of short stature. So he ran ahead and climbed up into a sycamore tree to see Him, for He was going to pass that way. And when Jesus came to the place, He looked up and saw him, and said to him, "Zacchaeus, make haste and come down, for today I must stay at your house." So he made haste and came down, and received Him joyfully. But when they saw it, they all complained, saying, "He has gone to be a guest with a man who is a sinner."

(Luke 19:1-7)

We have seen that in the eyes of man, Zacchaeus was a sinner but God loved him. Although the bible did not tell us that he has been praying for a long time, but I believe he did. He must have heard about Jesus from the people around him and when he heard that Jesus was passing through, he sought to see Him. The bible tells us that he ran on ahead and climbed up a sycamore tree to see Jesus because he was short. Probably many he has cheated might knock him in his head if he was to go and be mixed in the multitude to see Jesus. Jesus, who already knew that it would be so, saw him immediately.

And when Jesus came to the place, He looked up and saw him, and said to him, "Zacchaeus, make haste and come down, for today I must stay at your house." So he made haste and came down, and received Him joyfully.

(Luke 19:5-6)

Beloved, it does not matter how long you pray but what matters is how you pray and relate to God. I believe also that before Jesus told Zacchaeus to come down from the tree because He will be a guest in his house. Honestly, it was settled in heaven that Jesus was to be a guest at the house of Zacchaeus. Do you know why our Lord Jesus told Zacchaeus that He would be a guest at his house? It was because many were against him and Jesus wanted to wipe away his tears. May be he has fasted and cried out to God to see him through.

> But when they saw it, they all complained, saying, "He has gone to be a guest with a man who is a sinner." Then Zacchaeus stood and said to the Lord, "Look, Lord, I give half of my goods to the poor; and if I have taken anything from anyone by false accusation, I restore fourfold." And Jesus said to him, "Today salvation has come to this house, because he also is a son of Abraham; for the Son of Man has come to seek and to save that which was lost."
>
> (Luke 19:7-10)

We have seen what the people said about Zacchaeus. In the eyes of men, he was a sinner but God has forgiven him. Even though they might know him as someone who has asked God for forgiveness or someone who has repented from his sin, yet because of their envy towards him, they would speak against him.

Many who knew about my former life would keep reminding me of what I did in my former life when I was living in the flesh, even though they already knew that I have repented. They did that because of envy. They see how God has forgiven me and blessed me. Still, they will be saying it because of envy. I am not saying that it is not good to testify the kind of life we use to live when we repent, rather many will be saying it not to give God praise instead to distract others.

Beloved, be careful of this kind of people. They are in the church even in this end time.

Shall We Pray

Forever O LORD, Your Word is settled in heaven. Blessed be Your Holy Name. In Jesus name, I ask Thee O LORD to give me the grace to welcome anybody that comes my way. Give me the grace to love others, even those that do not have a good reputation.

Give me the ability to bring them to repentance. I do not walk by sight; rather I want to walk by faith. I do not want to be among those who ignore them who have bad reputations.

The bible says in 1 John 3:15-19, "Whoever hates his brother is a murderer, and you know that no murderer has eternal life abiding in him. By this we know love, because He laid down His life for us. And we also ought to lay down our lives for the brethren. But whoever has this world's goods, and sees his brother in need, and shuts up his heart from him, how does the love of God abide in him? My little children, let us not love in word or in tongue, but in deed and in truth. And by this we know that we are of the truth, and shall assure our hearts before Him."

In Jesus mighty name. Amen.

CHAPTER 5

THE WOMAN WITH THE ISSUE OF BLOOD

☙❧

Now a certain woman had a flow of blood for twelve years, and had suffered many things from many physicians. She had spent all that she had and was no better, but rather grew worse. When she heard about Jesus, she came behind Him in the crowd and touched His garment. For she said, "If only I may touch His clothes, I shall be made well." Immediately the fountain of her blood was dried up, and she felt in her body that she was healed of the affliction. And Jesus, immediately knowing in Himself that power had gone out of Him, turned around in the crowd and said, "Who touched My clothes?" But His disciples said to Him, "You see the multitude thronging You, and You say, 'Who touched Me?'" And He looked around to see her who had done this thing. But the woman, fearing and trembling, knowing what had happened to her, came and fell down before Him and told Him the whole truth. And He said to her, "Daughter, your faith has made you well. Go in peace, and be healed of your affliction."

(Mark 5:25-34)

Beloved I am going to explain the comprehensive meaning of this story to you. According to the Scripture in Mark 5:25-26 it says, *"Now a certain woman had a flow of blood for twelve years, and had suffered many things from many physicians. She had spent all that she had and was no better, but rather grew worse."*

Ladies and gentlemen, many are carried away by human ideas and methods. Many are deceived into thinking that doctors are the healers instead of God being the great Healer. And because of their weaknesses, they are easily deceived by human thoughts and ideas. Can you imagine, this woman has suffered from the issue of blood for twelve years? She could be a believer of Jesus Christ who has been praying for God to heal her for a long time. She could have gone to the physicians for healing but found no healing. In this end time, because of human mentality, many would advise her to put all her trust in the physicians for her healing. Do you know why I say that she could be a believer in the old days? Mark 5:34 says, *"And He said to her, "Daughter, your faith has made you well. Go in peace, and be healed of your affliction."*

Jesus said to her that her faith has made her well. But on many occasions, Jesus would say to those He has healed to sin no more.

> He answered them, "He who made me well said to me, 'Take up your bed and walk.'" Then they asked him, "Who is the Man who said to you, 'Take up your bed and walk'?" But the one who was healed did not know who it was, for Jesus had withdrawn, a multitude being in that place. Afterward Jesus found him in the temple, and said to him, *"See, you have been made well. Sin no more, lest a worse thing come upon you."*
>
> (John 5:11-14)

We have seen that Jesus told the man who was healed to sin no more. So, in the case of the woman who has the issue of blood, Jesus did not tell her to sin no more. Rather, Jesus told her that her faith has made her well. She could be a Christian in this end time, who because of the spirit of fear in her, she would not seek the face of Jesus through prayer and at the same time going to the doctors to receive her healing. Even in this end time church, many are carried away by human mentality and believe that there is no such thing as miracle in this present day. But let me tell you that the miracles of God still exist even today. God did many miracles in the past and He can surely do it again in this present day, because He is the same yesterday, today and forevermore. He is a miracle working God. Without the miracle of God, many will not be saved and believe that Jesus Christ is the Saviour and Lord.

> But one and the same Spirit works all these things, distributing to each one individually as He wills. For as the body is one and has many members, but all the members of that one body, being many, are one body, so also is Christ. For by one Spirit we were all baptized into one body—whether Jews or Greeks, whether slaves or free—and have all been made to drink into one Spirit.
> (1 Corinthians 12:11-13)

And God has appointed these in the church: first apostles, second prophets, third teachers, after that miracles, then gifts of healings, helps, administrations, varieties of tongues. Are all apostles? Are all prophets? Are all teachers? Are all workers of miracles? Do all have gifts of healings? Do all speak with tongues? Do all interpret? But earnestly desire the best gifts. And yet I show you a more excellent way.

(1 Corinthians 12:28-31)

Today, there are many independent churches who believe in the five-fold ministries. There are some who do not believe that the five-fold ministries still exist in this present time. Those who do not believe in it are opposing those who do believe in it. How can this be? The Scripture says in Ephesians 4:11, *"And He Himself gave some to be apostles, some prophets, some evangelists, and some pastors and teachers"*

The woman with the issue of blood may be one of those attending a church, which does not believe in the five-fold ministries. That was why for twelve years would have been going to the physicians for treatment and also spent all her money to get better.

And had suffered many things from many physicians. She had spent all that she had and was no better, but rather grew worse.

(Mark 5:26)

The bible tells us in Mark 5:27-29, "When she heard about Jesus, she came behind Him in the crowd and touched His garment. For she said, "If only I may touch His clothes, I shall be made well." Immediately the fountain of her blood was dried up, and she felt in her body that she was healed of the affliction."

We have seen how the woman went forward with unwavering faith to touch the garment of Jesus and she was healed. To the Jews, she would be considered unclean because of her blood flow. Everyone she touched became ceremonially unclean and she would not be welcome by society. However, she was willing to take the risk because she was desperate. Jesus was her only hope of getting healed. During the time of Jesus, there were many who truly believed that Jesus is the Son of God but there were also those who did not believe in Him. I hope you know what I am saying.

There were many who believed that Jesus is the Son of God but they would not say so because they were afraid of being thrown out of the synagogue by the Jews who were against Jesus.

> And they asked them, saying, "Is this your son, who you say was born blind? How then does he now see?" His parents answered them and

said, "We know that this is our son, and that he was born blind; but by what means he now sees we do not know, or who opened his eyes we do not know. He is of age; ask him. He will speak for himself." His parents said these things because they feared the Jews, for the Jews had agreed already that if anyone confessed that He was Christ, he would be put out of the synagogue. Therefore his parents said, "He is of age; ask him."

(John 9:19-23)

We have seen that the parents of the man who was healed of his blindness were afraid to answer for their son because they fear the Jews would not allow them to enter the synagogue if they were to say that it was Jesus Christ who healed their son. However, their son who was blind received his sight when Jesus healed him was not afraid to speak out what he knew. He was blind since birth and he must have suffered all those years. But now he was able to see and he was thankful to the person who healed him, not knowing at first that it was Jesus who has healed him. The bible tells us in John 9:35-38, "Jesus heard that they had cast him out; and when He had found him, He said to him, "Do you believe in the Son of God?" He answered and said, "Who is He, Lord, that I may believe in Him?"

And Jesus said to him, "You have both seen Him and it is He who is talking with you." Then he said, "Lord, I believe!" And he worshiped Him." So, in the case of the woman with the issue of the blood, she had a great need and had the faith to come to Jesus for its resolution because she believed that Jesus was able to heal her.

> And Jesus, immediately knowing in Himself that power had gone out of Him, turned around in the crowd and said, "Who touched My clothes?" But His disciples said to Him, "You see the multitude thronging You, and You say, 'Who touched Me?'" And He looked around to see her who had done this thing. But the woman, fearing and trembling, knowing what had happened to her, came and fell down before Him and told Him the whole truth.
>
> (Mark 5:30-33)

Ladies and gentlemen, how did she know that she would be healed immediately after she touched the garment of Jesus? That is what I am trying to explain. The woman believed that God is able to heal her, but there was no one at that time who was able to heal her. Probably she has gone to the physicians for the past twelve years but she was not getting healed but instead, her sickness must have grown worse. Take note that this woman knew her stand in God and she also knew her faith in God because Mark 5:33-34 tells us, *"But the woman, fearing and trembling, knowing what had happened to her, came and fell down before Him and told Him the whole truth. And He said to her, "Daughter, your faith has made you well. Go in peace, and be healed of your affliction."*

Beloved, the word in verse 33 really mean a lot. She came and fell down before Jesus and told Him the whole truth. I believe it was not only because she told the whole truth believing that she would receive her healing when she touched the garment of Jesus but she told Jesus she knew what to be done but she went and spend all that she had on the physicians for twelve years. I hope you understand what I am saying.

CHAPTER 6

RAHAB AND THE TWO SPIES

❦

Now Joshua the son of Nun sent out two men from Acacia Grove to spy secretly, saying, "Go, view the land, especially Jericho." So they went, and came to the house of a harlot named Rahab, and lodged there. And it was told the king of Jericho, saying, "Behold, men have come here tonight from the children of Israel to search out the country." So the king of Jericho sent to Rahab, saying, "Bring out the men who have come to you, who have entered your house, for they have come to search out all the country." Then the woman took the two men and hid them. So she said, "Yes, the men came to me, but I did not know where they were from. And it happened as the gate was being shut, when it was dark, that the men went out. Where the men went I do not know; pursue them quickly, for you may overtake them." (But she had brought them up to the roof and hidden them with the stalks of flax, which she had laid in order on the roof.) Then the men pursued them by the road to the Jordan, to the fords. And as soon as those who pursued them had gone out, they shut the gate.

Joshua 2:1-7

Beloved, this is one of the most interesting stories in the bible. Rahab was known as a harlot. What baffles me is that Jesus was from the descendant of Rahab. According to the Scripture in Matthew1:5 & 16 it says, "Salmon begot Boaz by Rahab, Boaz begot Obed by Ruth, Obed begot Jesse, and Jesse begot David the king. David the king begot Solomon by her who had been the wife of Uriah. *And Jacob begot Joseph the husband of Mary, of whom was born Jesus who is called Christ.*"

I am going to give the comprehensive meaning of the name RAHAB.

R Repent
A Abide
H Honour
A Appointed Time
B Believe

REPENT

Now before they lay down, she came up to them on the roof, and said to the men: "I know that the LORD has given you the land, that the terror of you has fallen on us, and that all the inhabitants of the land are fainthearted because of you. For we have heard how the LORD dried up the water of the Red Sea for you when you came out of Egypt, and what you did to the two kings of the Amorites who were on the other side of the Jordan, Sihon and Og, whom you utterly destroyed. And as soon as we heard these things, our hearts melted; neither did there remain any more courage in anyone because of you, for the LORD your God, He is God in heaven above and on earth beneath.

(Joshua 2:8-11)

Beloved, Apostle Peter said in 2 Peter 3:9-10, "The Lord is not slow in keeping his promise, as some understand slowness. He is patient with you, not wanting anyone to perish, but everyone to come to repentance. But the day of the Lord will come like a thief. The heavens will disappear with a roar; the elements will be destroyed by fire, and the earth and everything in it will be laid bare."

We have seen that Rahab was willing to see who will lead her to the Living God, but because of her reputation, she might be rejected by the people. However, God has not rejected her and the opportunity came for her and her family to be delivered by God's chosen people.

> For we have heard how the LORD dried up the water of the Red Sea for you when you came out of Egypt, and what you did to the two kings of the Amorites who were on the other side of the Jordan, Sihon and Og, whom you utterly destroyed. And as soon as we heard these things, our hearts melted; neither did there remain any more courage in anyone because of you, for the LORD your God, He is God in heaven above and on earth beneath.
> (Joshua 2:10-11)

We have seen that Rahab believed in the God of the people of Israel because she has heard what the God of Israel has done. When the opportunity came, she hid the two spies from their enemies and in return, she asked them to promise that she and her family's lives would be spared. Beloved, obedient to His Word is a price to greatness. It does not matter where you are but obedient to His leading will make you to prosper. When we see people like Rahab, we should not be quick to condemn them.

Once upon a time, I met a fellow Nigerian in one of the countries I used to stay. It happened that this man wanted to marry a prostitute. Every day we would meet and I would share the word of God with him. Before this, I did ask him whether he was willing for her to change and he said 'yes'. I also asked the woman whether she is willing to change and she said 'yes'.

However, to my greatest surprise, within that period all my countrymen shunned away from me when they heard that I was trying to convert a prostitute. Even those who said that they are pastors, they shunned from me. To me, it does not matter much to me whether men praise me or not. What matters most is the praise from God. Beloved, if you are going to make it to heaven, do not be carried away with people saying something against you. More so if you want to have a divine connection from God, let no one deceive you with empty words, for because of these things the wrath of God comes upon the sons of disobedience.

The bible tells us that Rahab was praising God because she has heard what God has done for the people of Israel.

And as soon as we heard these things, our hearts melted; neither did there remain any more courage in anyone because of you, for the LORD your God, He is God in heaven above and on earth beneath.
(Joshua 2:11)

Rahab gave God all the praise and adoration. She indeed believes that God is real and heaven is also real. I believe also that she has been praying for a long time, for God to deliver her and God did that at the appointed time. I was given a vision to preach to the prostitutes for a very long time, even the place I use to stay by them was where they use to hang around. Honestly, God really used me to set many prostitutes free. We don't have to fold our hands to see our beloved sisters perishing without making any effort to rescue them.

According to the scripture in 1 John 3:16-23, it says, "By this we know love, because He laid down His life for us. And we also ought to lay down our lives for the brethren. But whoever has this world's goods, and sees his brother in need, and shuts up his heart from him, how does the love of God abide in him? My little children, let us not love in word or in tongue, but in deed and in truth. And by this we know that we are of the truth, and shall assure our hearts before Him. For if our heart condemns us, God is greater than our heart, and knows all things. Beloved, if our heart does not condemn us, we have confidence toward God. And whatever we ask we receive from Him, because we keep His commandments and do those things that are pleasing in His sight. And this is His commandment: that we should believe on the name of His Son Jesus Christ and love one another, as He gave us commandment."

Brethren, if a man is overtaken in any trespass, you who are spiritual restore such a one in a spirit of gentleness, considering yourself lest you also be tempted. Bear one another's burdens, and so fulfil the law of Christ.

(Galatians 6:1-2)

Ladies and gentlemen, if you want to have a divine connection from God, bear one another's burden and fulfil the law of Christ. Do not neglect anyone.

ABIDE

He who dwells in the secret place of the Most High shall abide under the shadow of the Almighty. I will say of the LORD, "He is my refuge and my fortress, My God, in Him I will trust."

(Psalm 91:1-2)

Now therefore, I beg you, swear to me by the LORD, since I have shown you kindness, that you also will show kindness to my father's house, and give me a true token, and spare my father, my mother, my brothers, my sisters, and all that they have, and deliver our lives from death." So the men answered her, "Our lives for yours, if none of you tell this business of ours. And it shall be, when the LORD has given us the land, that we will deal kindly and truly with you." Then she let them down by a rope through the window, for her house was on the city wall; she dwelt on the wall.

(Joshua 2:12-15)

Beloved, we have seen that Rahab made a covenant with the two spies in the name of the Lord. In those days, to sincerely hold a covenant in the name of God is real. But in the present days, Jesus said in Matthew 5:33, "Again you have heard that it was said to those of old, 'You shall not swear falsely, but shall perform your oaths to the Lord.'"

And spare my father, my mother, my brothers, my sisters, and all that they have, and deliver our lives from death.
(Joshua 2:13)

What do you think that the parents of Rahab would say when she was doing the business of prostitution? Probably, she was rejected by her family because she did not show a good reputation. Even in this present day, many who said that they are Christians will be quick to condemn their daughters who are prostituting. Even, many would neglect them and would not preach to them the gospel for them to be saved. Many would gossip against them. Many would even reject them because they are prostitutes. It does not work like that. Love is blind and to love is to live.

Honestly, the bible did not say it in vain that the greatest commandment is love. Jesus said, "If you keep My commandments, you will abide in My love, just as I have kept My Father's commandments and abide in His love. "These things I have spoken to you, that My joy may remain in you, and that your joy may be full. This is My commandment, that you love one another as I have loved you. *Greater love has no one than this, than to lay down one's life for his friends.*"

According to the bible in John 8:3-11 says, "Then the scribes and Pharisees brought to Him a woman caught in adultery. And when they had set her in the midst, they said to Him, "Teacher, this woman was caught in adultery, in the very act. Now Moses, in the law, commanded us that such should be stoned. But what do You say?" This they said, testing Him, that they might have something of which to accuse Him. But Jesus stooped down and wrote on the ground with His finger, as though He did not hear. So when they continued asking Him, He raised Himself up and said to them, "He who is without sin among you, let him throw a stone at her first." And again He stooped down and wrote on the ground. Then those who heard it, being convicted by their conscience, went out one by one, beginning with the oldest even to the last. And Jesus was left alone, and the woman standing in the midst. When Jesus had raised Himself up and saw no one but the woman, He said to her, "Woman, where are those accusers of yours? Has no one condemned you?" She said, "No one, Lord." And Jesus said to her, "Neither do I condemn you; go and sin no more.""

Beloved, do not condemn anyone for God so loved the world that He gave His only Begotten Son, Jesus to die for our sin. Above all, Jesus said "Abide in Me, and I in you. As the branch cannot bear fruit of itself, unless it abides in the vine, neither can you, unless you abide in Me. "I am the vine, you are the branches. He who abides in Me, and I in him, bears much fruit; for without Me you can do nothing. If anyone does not abide in Me, he is cast out as a branch and is withered; and they gather them and throw them into the fire, and they are burned. If you abide in Me, and My words abide in you, you will ask what you desire, and it shall be done for you. By this My Father is glorified, that you bear much fruit; so you will be My disciples. "As the Father loved Me, I also have loved you; abide in My love. If you keep My commandments, you will abide in My love, just as I have kept My Father's commandments and abide in His love. "These things I have spoken to you, that My joy may remain in you, and that your joy may be full."

HONOUR

Restore us, O God of hosts. Cause Your face to shine, And we shall be saved Then we will not turn back from You, Revive us, and we will call upon Your name. Restore us, O LORD God of hosts, Cause Your face to shine, And we shall be saved.
(Psalm 80:7& 18-19)

And she said to them, "Get to the mountain, lest the pursuers meet you. Hide there three days, until the pursuers have returned. Afterward you may go your way." So the men said to her: "We will be blameless of this oath of yours which you have made us swear, unless, when we come into the land, you bind this line of scarlet cord in the window through which you let us down, and unless you bring your father, your mother, your brothers, and all your father's household to your own home. So it shall be that whoever goes outside the doors of your house into the street, his blood shall be on his own head, and we will be guiltless. And whoever is with you in the house, his blood shall be on our head if a hand is laid on him. And if you tell this business of ours, then we will be free from your oath which you made us swear." Then she said, "According to your words, so be it." And she sent them away, and they departed. And she bound the scarlet cord in the window. They departed and went to the mountain, and stayed there three days until the pursuers returned. The pursuers sought them all along the way, but did not find them. So the two men returned, descended from the mountain, and crossed over; and they came to Joshua the son of Nun, and told him all that had befallen them. And they said to Joshua, "Truly the LORD has delivered all the land into our hands, for indeed all the inhabitants of the country are fainthearted because of us."

(Joshua 2:16-24)

Beloved, when you read the whole story about Rahab and the two spies, you will see that the two spies did keep their word with Rahab. So, Rahab and her family's lives were saved. Joshua 6:15-17, "But it came to pass on the seventh day that they rose early, about the dawning of the day, and marched around the city seven times in the same manner. On that day only they marched around the city seven times. And the seventh time it happened, when the priests blew the trumpets, that Joshua said to the people: "Shout, for the LORD has given you the city! Now the city shall be doomed by the

LORD to destruction, it and all who are in it. Only Rahab the harlot shall live, she and all who are with her in the house, because she hid the messengers that we sent."

Beloved, there is a need to honour God's word. But today, many do not keep what they say to their fellow brothers or sisters. We have seen that the two spies sent by Joshua to spy on Jericho did keep their promise and that is what we need to do in this present time.

Let us see what the bible says in Joshua 6:22-25, "But Joshua had said to the two men who had spied out the country, "Go into the harlot's house, and from there bring out the woman and all that she has, as you swore to her." And the young men who had been spies went in and brought out Rahab, her father, her mother, her brothers, and all that she had. So they brought out all her relatives and left them outside the camp of Israel. But they burned the city and all that was in it with fire. Only the silver and gold, and the vessels of bronze and iron, they put into the treasury of the house of the LORD. And Joshua spared Rahab the harlot, her father's household, and all that she had. So she dwells in Israel to this day, because she hid the messengers whom Joshua sent to spy out Jericho."

Let the elders who rule well be counted worthy of double honour, especially those who labour in the word and doctrine.

(1 Timothy 5:17)

APPOINTED TIME

To everything there is a season, a time for every purpose under heaven.

(Ecclesiastes 3:1)

Beloved, Rahab was one of the heroes in the bible, who risked her life regardless of what she would go through. She believed there is a Living God who was able to deliver her at the appointed time. As I have mentioned to you earlier in Joshua 2:11, *"And as soon as we heard these things, our hearts melted; neither did there remain any more courage in anyone because of you, for the LORD your God, He is God in heaven above and on earth beneath."*

Beloved, today many are praising men but when it is time to praise God, they will not be interested. Do you know that Rahab said to the spies, "For the Lord your God, He is God in heaven above and on earth beneath", and that has made God to save her and her family's lives. She also said in Joshua 2:12-13, *"Now therefore, I beg you, swear to me by the LORD, since I have shown you kindness, that you also will show kindness to my father's house, and give me a true token, and spare my father, my mother, my brothers, my sisters, and all that they have, and deliver our lives from death."*

Do you know, if she did not save the lives of the two spies and had it been that the king of Jericho discovered that the two spies were hiding in Rahab's house, what do you think would have happened? They would have lost their lives. Beloved, God is concerned where He is leading us. If it is the will of God for you to help or save someone's life that has been rejected by the people, honour Him by helping the person. If it is the will of God for you to help a non-believer, do it with all pleasure.

Do not be carried away about what people are saying about anyone. Rather believe that one day God will remember you, just as He saved the life of Rahab and her family. Beloved, do you know only Rahab and her family and household were saved by the people of Israel when they destroyed Jericho and all the men and women in it.

Now the city shall be doomed by the LORD to destruction, it and all who are in it. Only Rahab the harlot shall live, she and all who are with her in the house, because she hid the messengers that we sent.

(Joshua 6:17)

Beloved, he who endures shall be saved. Heaven and earth shall pass away but His word will remain the same. Believe in God, even though you may be the only Christian in a country where you are staying. Believe that one day, God will deliver you as He did with Rahab and her family. Do not be deceived by anyone and do not be double minded.

BELIEVE

If you confess with your mouth the Lord Jesus and believe in your heart that God has raised Him from the dead, you will be saved. For with the heart one believes unto righteousness, and with the mouth confession is made unto salvation. For the Scripture says, "Whoever believes on Him will not be put to shame." For there is no distinction between Jew and Greek, for the same Lord over all is rich to all who call upon Him. For "whoever calls on the name of the LORD shall be saved." How then shall they call on Him in whom they have not believed? And how shall they believe in Him of whom they have not heard? And how shall they hear without a preacher?

(Romans 10:9-14)

Beloved, we have seen that Rahab believed in God and God really proved to her that He is a God of miracles.

For what does the Scripture say? "Abraham believed God, and it was accounted to him for righteousness."

(Romans 4:3)

Rahab believed God and I believe that she has been longing to witness more about God for a very long time. God really remembered her. I also believe that although she was a harlot, she was looking who will deliver her from that problem.

And certain women who had been healed of evil spirits and infirmities—Mary called Magdalene, out of whom had come seven demons, and Joanna the wife of Chuza, Herod's steward, and Susanna, and many others who provided for Him from their substance.

(Luke 8:2-3)

Jesus delivered Mary Magdalene from seven demons. What baffles me though, was Mary Magdalene was also among those who supported the ministry of Jesus Christ. *At the same time, she was the first person who saw Jesus at the tomb after His resurrection.*

> Mary Magdalene came and told the disciples that she had seen the Lord, and that He had spoken these things to her. Then, the same day at evening, being the first day of the week, when the doors were shut where the disciples were assembled, for fear of the Jews, Jesus came and stood in the midst, and said to them, "Peace be with you."
>
> (John 20:18-19)

We have seen in the above verse that the disciples were staying indoors because they were afraid of the Jews. When Jesus came and stood in their midst and greeted them, the disciples were glad as they witnessed the resurrection power of Jesus and they were encouraged.

CHAPTER 7

LAZARUS COME FORTH

༄༅

Now when He had said these things, He cried with a loud voice, "Lazarus, come forth!" And he who had died came out bound hand and foot with grave clothes, and his face was wrapped with a cloth. Jesus said to them, "Loose him, and let him go."

(John 11:43-44)

Beloved, Jesus said in Matthew 5:3-9, "Blessed are the poor in spirit, for theirs is the kingdom of heaven. Blessed are those who mourn, for they shall be comforted. Blessed are the meek, for they shall inherit the earth. Blessed are those who hunger and thirst for righteousness, for they shall be filled. Blessed are the merciful, for they shall obtain mercy. Blessed are the pure in heart, for they shall see God. Blessed are the peacemakers, for they shall be called sons of God."

We have seen that Jesus loved Lazarus, Martha and Mary as mentioned in John 11:5, "Now Jesus loved Martha and her sister and Lazarus." When the bible declares that Jesus, our Saviour loved someone, honestly it means a lot to me. We know that there is no partiality in God because when God loves you, it is one of the greatest miracles. For example, the bible says in John 13:23, *"Now there was leaning on Jesus' bosom one of His disciples, whom Jesus loved."*

> And Simon Peter followed Jesus, and so did another disciple. Now that disciple was known to the high priest, and went with Jesus into the courtyard of the high priest. But Peter stood at the door outside. Then the other disciple, who was known to the high priest, went out and spoke to her who kept the door, and brought Peter in.
>
> (John 18:15-16)

We have seen that all the disciples except John forsook Him and fled. John did not deny Jesus like Peter did. He was known by the high priest. Do you know, before Jesus was crucified, He already loved John? (John 13:23)

Beloved, when God loves you, to me it means according to the Scripture in Psalm 32:1-11.

PRAYER FOR GOD'S BLESSING

Shall We Pray

Blessed is he whose transgression is forgiven, whose sin is covered. Blessed is the man to whom the LORD does not impute iniquity, and in whose spirit there is no deceit. When I kept silent, my bones grew old through my groaning all the day long. For day and night, Your hand was heavy upon me; my vitality was turned into the drought of summer. Selah I acknowledged my sin to You, and my iniquity I have not hidden. I said, "I will confess my transgressions to the LORD," And You forgave the iniquity of my sin. Selah For this cause everyone who is godly shall pray to You in a time when You may be found; surely in a flood of great waters they shall not come near him. You are my hiding place; You shall preserve me from trouble; You shall surround me with songs of deliverance. Selah I will instruct you and teach you in the way you should go; I will guide you with My eye. Do not be like the horse or like the mule, which have no understanding, which must be harnessed with bit and bridle, else they will not come near you. Many sorrows shall be to the wicked; but he who trusts in the LORD, mercy shall surround him. Be glad in the

LORD and rejoice, you righteous; and shout for joy, all you upright in heart! In Jesus mighty name we pray.

According to the story, Martha, Mary and Lazarus their brother deeply loved Jesus. These were the people whose 'yes' is yes. They were willing to spend all they had for His namesake.

It was that Mary, the sister of Lazarus, who anointed the Lord with fragrant oil and wiped His feet with her hair.

(John 11:2)

Then Mary took a pound of very costly oil of spikenard, anointed the feet of Jesus, and wiped His feet with her hair and the house was filled with the fragrance of the oil.

(John 12:3)

Beloved, do you know how much 300 denarii will cost in this end time? It would have cost thousands of dollars in this present time. Yet, Mary the sister of Lazarus has the courage to pour it on Jesus. Beloved, we cannot just expect Jesus to love us while we are not giving something tangible to Him. Are you a friend of God?

For what does the Scripture say? "Abraham believed God, and it was accounted to him for righteousness." Blessed are those whose lawless deeds are forgiven, and whose sins are covered
(Romans 4:3 & 7)

Indeed Abraham was a friend of God and that was why Apostle Paul said in Galatians 3:7 & 29, "Therefore know that only those who are of faith are sons of Abraham. And if you are Christ's, then you are Abraham's seed, and heirs according to the promise."

Beloved, are you highly recognized by God or men? We have seen that Abraham walked in the steps of righteousness and that was why God made him the father of all nations.

> (as it is written, "I have made you a father of many nations") in the presence of Him whom he believed—God, who gives life to the dead and calls those things which do not exist as though they did; who, contrary to hope, in hope believed, so that he became the father of many nations, according to what was spoken, "So shall your descendants be."
> (Romans 4:17-18)

I believe God knows what to be done for His faithful ones in Jesus' name.

Then Jesus said to them plainly, "Lazarus is dead."
(John 11:14)

Now Martha said to Jesus, "Lord, if You had been here, my brother would not have died. But even now I know that whatever You ask of God, God will give You." Jesus said to her, "Your brother will rise again." Martha said to Him, "I know that he will rise again in the resurrection at the last day." Jesus said to her, "I am the resurrection and the life. He who believes in Me, though he may die, he shall live. And whoever lives and believes in Me shall never die. Do you believe this?" She said to Him, "Yes, Lord, I believe that You are the Christ, the Son of God, who is to come into the world."
(John 11:21-27)

There are several points that we can take note. The family of Lazarus believed that Jesus is the Son of God and they also believed that God really used Jesus to raise Lazarus from the dead. They did not have any doubt about Him.

Martha said to Him, "I know that he will rise again in the resurrection at the last day." Jesus said to her, "I am the resurrection and the life. He who believes in Me, though he may die, he shall live. And whoever lives and believes in Me shall never die. Do you believe this?" She said to Him, "Yes, Lord, I believe that You are the Christ, the Son of God, who is to come into the world."

(John 11:24-27)

They believed that Jesus is really the Son of God. They believed that there is life after death. Jesus loved them and because of their faithfulness, He was willing to perform a tremendous miracle in their midst. You know there are many Christians who have been in the faith for over twenty years, but still, they do not believe that there is life after death. There are also many Christians who are double minded. There are many who believe that the world is heaven and earth.

Jesus said to her, "Did I not say to you that if you would believe you would see the glory of God?"

(John 11:40)

I understand from this story that Lazarus, Martha and Mary were also part of the ministry of Jesus in Bethany. Many came to believe in Jesus because they saw how Jesus raised Lazarus from the dead.

Then many of the Jews who had come to Mary, and had seen the things Jesus did, believed in Him.

(John 11:45)

But the chief priests plotted to put Lazarus to death also, because on account of him many of the Jews went away and believed in Jesus.

(John 12:10-11)

Beloved, did you think that Lazarus, whom Jesus raised from the dead would not be representing the ministry of Jesus in Bethany? Honestly, many would be coming to see him for prayer. Do you understand what I am saying? Lazarus has been dead for four days and Jesus raised him from the dead. Of course God has called him into the ministry already. But today many will be waiting until God comes down from heaven they will know that they are called to do God's work when such tremendous miracles happen to them. Ladies and gentlemen, let us be honest with ourselves. When such a tremendous miracle happens to us, are we going to fold our hands? Off course not, if you want to have a divine connection from God, believe that every day in your life is a testimony because many sleep without waking up from their bed. I hope you understand want I am saying. We should be enthusiastic to be a part of God's kingdom business of bringing as many souls as we can into His kingdom. Winning souls for the kingdom of God is the greatest task given to us by God, especially in this end time. The bible tells us, "For God so loved the world that He gave His only begotten Son, that whoever believes in Him should not perish but have everlasting life."

All who believe in Jesus Christ will go through trials and temptation. But God, who is faithful beyond temptation, will not allow you to be defeated. Whether he or she is in full time ministry or not, he or she must be willing to sacrifice for His namesake. I believe Lazarus would hold meetings in his house and many would come and be ministered and believed in Jesus. Beloved, if you want to have a divine connection from God, you need to be a Lazarus of this end time. This word is a challenge to you. If you are among those God has delivered from a serious problem, what are doing for Him in return?

I have a friend who got shot by many bullets for trafficking cocaine in America. He was badly wounded but he survived. And because of that, he gave his life to Jesus. He would give his testimony about what God was doing in his life at every opportunity given to him. However, later he backslid and had a terrible sickness. It seemed that he would not survive from sickness. I went to the hospital to see him and I cried out to God on his behalf to give him a second chance. Within that period, he was delivered from sickness. Do you know even the doctors were amazed that he could survive from the sickness he had? However, after he recovered from his sickness, he went back to his formal lifestyle and has stopped going to church. He was busy chasing women, drinking and smoking. He was also a drug addict. So, within that period I had a dream that he died. I went to him and told him about it but he would not listen to me. Even before that period of time, whenever he drinks and smoke, he would be reacting strangely. I discovered that God was showing him a sign that he was going to die. To make a long story short, the young man died a shameful death exactly one year after I told him the dream I had, that he was going to die.

A man's gift makes room for him, and brings him before great men.

(Proverbs 18:16)

PRAYER FOR GOD TO USE YOU

Shall We Pray

Forever O LORD Your Word says that unless the LORD builds the house, they labour in vain who build it; unless the LORD guards the city, the watchman stays awake in vain. Use me O LORD to raise a dead man, so that those who are looking down on me will be ashamed of themselves. Use me O LORD to perform tremendous miracles, so that those who do not believe in You might come to believe in You because the bible says that we can do all things through Christ who strengthens us.

John 14:12-14 says, ""Most assuredly, I say to you, he who believes in Me, the works that I do he will do also; and greater works than these he will do, because I go to My Father. And whatever you ask in My name, that I will do, that the Father may be glorified in the Son. If you ask anything in My name, I will do it."

I ask all these through Jesus Christ our LORD. Amen.

CHAPTER 8

ESTHER AND MORDECAI

ೂ

Beloved, this is one of the most interesting stories in the bible. The story between Mordecai and Haman was like a story between God and the devil. But the most interesting thing in this story was that Mordecai was a man of integrity, whose 'yes' is yes.

According to the story in Esther 3:1-6 says, "After these things King Ahasuerus promoted Haman, the son of Hammedatha the Agagite, and advanced him and set his seat above all the princes who were with him. And all the king's servants who were within the king's gate bowed and paid homage to Haman, for so the king had commanded concerning him. But Mordecai would not bow or pay homage. Then the king's servants who were within the king's gate said to Mordecai, "Why do you transgress the king's command?" Now it happened, when they spoke to him daily and he would not listen to them, that they told it to Haman, to see whether Mordecai's words would stand; for Mordecai had told them that he was a Jew. When Haman saw that Mordecai did not bow or pay him homage, Haman was filled with wrath. But he disdained to lay hands on Mordecai alone, for they had told him of the people of Mordecai. Instead, Haman sought to destroy all the Jews who were throughout the whole kingdom of Ahasuerus—the people of Mordecai."

In Esther 3:8-11 says, "Then Haman said to King Ahasuerus, "There is a certain people scattered and dispersed among the people in all the provinces of your kingdom; their laws are different from all other people's, and they do not keep the king's laws. Therefore it is not fitting for the king to let them remain. If it pleases the king, let a decree be written that they be destroyed, and I will pay ten thousand talents of silver into the hands of those who do the work, to bring it into the king's treasuries." So the king took his signet ring from his hand and gave it to Haman, the son of Hammedatha the Agagite, the enemy of the Jews. And the king said to Haman, "The money and the people are given to you, to do with them as seems good to you." In so many occasions, Mordecai did not bow down to Haman. Beloved, we can learn a lesson from this story. Even though the decree has been made, still Mordecai did not bow down to Haman.

So Hathach returned and told Esther the words of Mordecai. Then Esther spoke to Hathach, and gave him a command for Mordecai: "All the king's servants and the people of the king's provinces know that any man or woman who goes into the inner court to the king, who has not been called, he has but one law: put all to death, except the one to whom the king holds out the golden sceptre, that he may live. Yet I myself have not been called to go in to the king these thirty days." So they told Mordecai Esther's words. And Mordecai told them to answer Esther: "Do not think in your heart that you will escape in the king's palace any more than all the other Jews. For if you remain completely silent at this time, relief and deliverance will arise for the Jews from another place, but you and your father's house will perish. Yet who knows whether you have come to the kingdom for such a time as this?"

(Esther 4:9-14)

We have seen, even though it meant that Mordecai would lose his life for not bowing down to Haman, Mordecai would not do so. It is just like bowing down to the devil. Beloved, be strong in the Lord and in the power of His might. Put on the Armor of God so that you may be able to withstand in the evil day. God wants to see us facing challenges when it comes.

Honestly, when we begin to face the challenges when it comes along our way, it is when God will come to us or appear to us. So, we have seen that God is willing to see us through when we face every challenge that comes. Ladies and gentlemen, behave as a child of God should and fear not because life in this world is very short.

For a thousand years in Your sight are like yesterday when it is past, and like a watch in the night. The days of our lives are seventy years; and if by reason of strength they are eighty years, yet their boast is only labour and sorrow; for it is soon cut off, and we fly away.
(Psalm 90:4 & 10)

Then Esther told them to reply to Mordecai: "Go, gather all the Jews who are present in Shushan, and fast for me; neither eat nor drink for three days, night or day. My maids and I will fast likewise. And so I will go to the king, which is against the law; and if I perish, I perish!"

(Esther 4:15-16)

What would you do if you were put in a similar situation, where you and your family's lives are threatened because of your obedience to God? Beloved, when we enlarge our faith in God, we become overcomers and winners. Do you know that there are benefits in fasting? According to the law at that time, nobody has the right to see the king unless he or she was summoned by the king. Esther knew that whoever appeared before the king without being summoned by the king would be killed unless the king holds out his sceptre. Even though she was the Queen she had no right to appear before the king to plead on behalf of her people. Nevertheless, after she and the Jews had fasted for three days, she took courage and went to see the king.

> Now it happened on the third day that Esther put on her royal robes and stood in the inner court of the king's palace, across from the king's house, while the king sat on his royal throne in the royal house, facing the entrance

of the house. So it was, when the king saw Queen Esther standing in the court that she found favour in his sight, and the king held out to Esther the golden sceptre that was in his hand. Then Esther went near and touched the top of the sceptre. And the king said to her, "What do you wish, Queen Esther? What is your request? It shall be given to you—up to half the kingdom!" So Esther answered, "If it pleases the king, let the king and Haman come today to the banquet that I have prepared for him." Then the king said, "Bring Haman quickly, that he may do as Esther has said." So the king and Haman went to the banquet that Esther had prepared. At the banquet of wine the king said to Esther, "What is your petition? It shall be granted you. What is your request, up to half the kingdom? It shall be done!" Then Esther answered and said, "My petition and request is this: If I have found favour in the sight of the king, and if it pleases the king to grant my petition and fulfil my request, then let the king and Haman come to the banquet which I will prepare for them, and tomorrow I will do as the king has said."

(Esther 5:1-8)

Remember Mordecai, he was one of those who sat within the king's gate. When it was made known to him that two of the king's eunuchs, Bigthan and Teresh wanted to lay hands on King Ahasuerus because they were furious with the king, he told Queen Esther about it. Queen Esther was his niece whom he had brought up when her parents died. So Queen Esther informed the king, in Mordecai's name. However, no honour was bestowed upon Mordecai for his service.

One night, the king was restless and commanded his men to bring the book of records of the chronicles and to read them to him. It was then that the king remembered what Mordecai had done for him. The king was wondering how he could reward Mordecai. The king asked his servant who was in the court. At that time Haman, who hated Mordecai because he did not bow to him whenever he saw him passing, happened to be in the court. So the king summoned for him to come before his presence. When Haman came the king asked him "What shall be done for the man whom the king delights to honour?" Haman thought that the king was referring to him. So he said to the king, "Let a royal robe be brought which the king has worn, and a horse on which the king has ridden, which has a royal crest placed on its head. Then let this robe and horse be delivered to the hand of one of the king's most noble princes, that he may array the man whom the king delights to honour. Then parade him on horseback through the city square, and proclaim before him; 'Thus shall be done to the man whom the king delights to honour!'" The king then told Haman to do exactly what he has recommended towards Mordecai immediately. Can you imagine how Haman must have felt when he found out that the king was actually referring to Mordecai and not him?

Haman was a rich man in the eyes of man. He hated Mordecai, a Jew because he did not want to bow down to him. He sought to destroy all the Jews who were throughout the kingdom and he even offered to pay ten thousand talents to have the Jews destroyed. To make a long story short, they hanged Haman on the gallows that he had prepared for Mordecai. (Esther 7:10) In the end, Mordecai the Jew won and defeated his plans and later became second in command to King Ahasuerus. Esther 10:3 says, *"For Mordecai the Jews was the second to King Ahasuerus, and was great among the Jews and well received by the multitude of his brethren, seeking the good of his people and speaking peace to all his countrymen."*

Above all, God used Queen Esther to save the lives of Mordecai and all the Jews. The bible tells us in Esther 2:5-11, "In Shushan the citadel there was a certain Jew whose name was Mordecai the son of Jair, the son of Shimei, the son of Kish, a Benjamite. Kish had been carried away from Jerusalem with the captives who had been captured with Jeconiah king of Judah, whom Nebuchadnezzar the king of Babylon had carried away. And Mordecai had brought up Hadassah, that is, Esther, his uncle's daughter, for she had neither father nor mother. The young woman was lovely and beautiful. When her father and mother died, Mordecai took her as his own daughter. So it was, when the king's command and decree were heard, and when many young women were gathered at Shushan the citadel, under the custody of Hegai, that Esther also was taken to the king's palace, into the care of Hegai the custodian of the women. Now the young woman pleased him, and she obtained his favour; so he readily gave beauty preparations to her, besides her allowance. Then seven choice maidservants were provided for her from the king's palace, and he moved her and her maidservants to the best place in the house of the women. Esther had not revealed her people or family, for Mordecai had charged her not to reveal it. And every day Mordecai paced in front of the court of the women's quarters, to learn of Esther's welfare and what was happening to her.

CHAPTER 9

MY JOURNEY TO CHINA

❧

In 2006, the Lord spoke to me to go to China. I went there for the first time with my wife. Honestly, I did not know anyone in China. Therefore, one day my wife and I went to the market to buy something but we did not know what bus to catch to go back to our hotel. We met a man who happened to be my fellow countryman and he told us what bus to take, not knowing that he was my brother-in-law that I have never met before. I found out about it when I introduced myself to him. When he found out who I was, he called his pastor and introduced me to him. His pastor invited us to come to his office and we did. He told me that he would be holding a big program called Open Heaen in twenty-one days and would like me to come and preach. He was a pastor of a big church and in his church, there were many pastors waiting to have the opportunity to preach in the church but to God be the glory because I am God sent to him. However, I was given the opportunity to preach in his church for almost one week because God was involved in my coming to China.

Also I heard the voice of the Lord, saying: "Whom shall I send, and who will go for Us?" Then I said, "Here am I! Send me."

(Isaiah 6:8)

Beloved, God is looking for those who are available. Are you available for God to use you? When we are willing and obedient to His Word, we shall eat the good of the land. God knows the hearts of His people.

Today, many are called to travel to far places to preach the gospel but they would not obey Him because they would not be receiving any monthly salary from the local church there.

> "Now it shall come to pass, if you diligently obey the voice of the LORD your God, to observe carefully all His commandments which I command you today, that the LORD your God will set you high above all nations of the earth. And all these blessings shall come upon you and overtake you, because you

obey the voice of the LORD your God: "Blessed shall you be in the city, and blessed shall you be in the country. "Blessed shall be the fruit of your body, the produce of your ground and the increase of your herds, the increase of your cattle and the offspring of your flocks. "Blessed shall be your basket and your kneading bowl. "Blessed shall you be when you come in, and blessed shall you be when you go out. "The LORD will cause your enemies who rise against you to be defeated before your face; they shall come out against you one way and flee before you seven ways.
(Deuteronomy 28:1-7)

My life is full of testimonies ever since God called me into the ministry. Instead of the churches in my hometown and abroad supporting me, I would be supporting them. Honestly, God never fail me in the ministry because I know what the bible says.

Do you not know that those who minister the holy things eat of the things of the temple, and those who serve at the altar partake of the offerings of the altar? Even so, the Lord has commanded that those who preach the gospel should live from the gospel.
(1 Corinthians 9:13-14)

I have been living in faith ever since God has called me into the ministry. Honestly, God provides for all my needs and I am not in lack. I do not even have to go to the hospital anymore because God keeps me in good health as I continue to serve Him faithfully. He has given me the grace to overcome every obstacle that may come my way, in the mighty name of Jesus.

When God calls us into the ministry, we should not give the excuse that we are not doing what He has called to do because we do not know what to do.

For if I preach the gospel, I have nothing to boast of, for necessity is laid upon me; yes, woe is me if I do not preach the gospel! For if I do this willingly, I have a reward; but if against my will, I have been entrusted with a stewardship.
(1 Corinthians 9:16-17)

Today, many will not go out to preach in the street. Rather, they only want to preach to the congregation in a church where they will be receiving a monthly salary. If it is the will of God for you to preach in the church, then there is no problem. However, many preachers are given the privilege to preach in the church because of their influence, while those who are supposed to be there will not be given the opportunity to preach there.

This wisdom I have also seen under the sun, and it seemed great to me: There was a little city with few men in it; and a great king came against it, besieged it, and built great snares around it. Now there was found in it a poor wise man and he by his wisdom delivered the city. Yet no one remembered that same poor man.
(Ecclesiastes 9:13-14-15)

That is why today, many are suffering from one sickness or another and they are in the various churches of this end time. When we occupy our position, our good God will see us through. Do you think God will be happy if we are to occupy another person's position? Honestly, when we know that God has called us into a ministry but we have not yet discovered what He wants us to do, we should start preaching and sharing the Word of God with others especially those who do not know Christ and at the same time continue to seek His face for His divine direction.

Preach the word! Be ready in season and out of season. Convince, rebuke, exhort, with all long suffering and teaching.

(2 Timothy 4:2)

Many preachers are occupying positions that do not belong to them because of the salaries they are receiving.

For the love of money is a root of all kinds of evil, for which some have strayed from the faith in their greediness, and pierced themselves through with many sorrows. But you, O man of God, flee these things and pursue righteousness, godliness, faith, love, patience, gentleness. Fight the good fight of faith, lay hold on eternal life, to which you were also called and have confessed the good confession in the presence of many witnesses.

(1 Timothy 6:10-12)

If you want to have a divine connection from God, seek first the kingdom of God and all these things will be added to you. Honestly, I have seen many who are not interested to preach in a church if they are not being paid. My greatest surprise is, there are many preachers who know what it takes to make it to heaven but they would rather put their focus on money instead of waiting on God. I used to hold church services in a garage every day back in my hometown. God told me to go there to preach. At that time, I was still a young preacher, growing in the ministry. Besides, there were many preachers who were doing the same thing within that area because there were many garages there. So one day, I asked several preachers who used to assist me to take over because I was busy trying to get my travelling documents so that I could travel to overseas. But they insisted that they must receive their salary from the owner of the garage. However, when I was there the owner saw my heart and every week he would give to me something of great valued. I did not have to demand it from him. I was disappointed by my fellow preachers because none of them was interested to preach there unless they are being paid.

Beloved, do you know that the eyes of God are on His chosen ones. He does not like His chosen ones to focus on demanding rather he want to see us obeying his word. Remember that King Solomon asked God to give him wisdom and God gave him more than what he asks for.

> Therefore give to Your servant an understanding heart to judge Your people, that I may discern between good and evil. For

who is able to judge this great people of Yours?" The speech pleased the Lord, that Solomon had asked this thing. Then God said to him: "Because you have asked this thing, and have not asked long life for yourself, nor have asked riches for yourself, nor have asked the life of your enemies, but have asked for yourself understanding to discern justice, behold, I have done according to your words; see, I have given you a wise and understanding heart, so that there has not been anyone like you before you, nor shall any like you arise after you. And I have also given you what you have not asked: both riches and honour, so that there shall not be anyone like you among the kings all your days.

1 Kings 3:9-13

Shall We Pray

Forever O LORD Your Word says "I heard the voice of the Lord, saying: "Whom shall I send, and who will go for Us?" Then I said, "Here am I! Send me."

O LORD I am willing to go wherever You send me, even though it is to the most difficult place, I ask You to give me the grace to endure because the bible says in 1 Corinthians 9:16-17, *"For if I preach the gospel, I have nothing to boast of, for necessity is laid upon me; yes, woe is me if I do not preach the gospel! For if I do this willingly, I have a reward; but if against my will, I have been entrusted with a stewardship."*

In Jesus mighty name. Amen.

CHAPTER 10

CORNELIUS AND APOSTLE PETER

❧

While Peter was still speaking these words, the Holy Spirit fell upon all those who heard the word. And those of the circumcision who believed were astonished, as many as came with Peter, because the gift of the Holy Spirit had been poured out on the Gentiles also. For they heard them speak with tongues and magnify God. Then Peter answered, "Can anyone forbid water, that these should not be baptized who have received the Holy Spirit just as we have?" And he commanded them to be baptized in the name of the Lord. Then they asked him to stay a few days.

(Acts 10:44-48)

Beloved, this is an interesting story. According to the bible in Acts 10:1-8 it says, "There was a certain man in Caesarea called Cornelius, a centurion of what was called the Italian Regiment, a devout man and one who feared God with all his household, who gave alms generously to the people, and prayed to God always. About the ninth hour of the day he saw clearly in a vision an angel of God coming in and saying to him, "Cornelius!" And when he observed him, he was afraid, and said, "What is it, lord?" So he said to him, "Your prayers and your alms have come up for a memorial before God. Now send men to Joppa, and send for Simon whose surname is Peter. He is lodging with Simon, a tanner, whose house is by the sea. He will tell you what you must do." And when the angel who spoke to him had departed, Cornelius called two of his household servants and a devout soldier from among those who waited on him continually. So when he had explained all these things to them, he sent them to Joppa."

The Scripture says that this man called Cornelius was a centurion of the Italian regiment. A centurion usually has an army of eighty to one hundred soldiers under his command. He has the power to promote or punish his subordinates. Nevertheless, the bible tells us that he was a devout man and one who feared God together with his household, who gave alms generously to the people and prayed to God always. Do you know there are many like him in this end time that holds great authority and because of their title, they would not be interested to put their trust in God. Jesus said in Luke 18:22-25, "So when Jesus heard these things, He said to him, "You still lack one thing. Sell all that you have and distribute to the poor, and you will have treasure in heaven; and come, follow Me." But when he heard this, he became very sorrowful, for he was very rich. And when Jesus saw that he became very sorrowful, He said, "How hard it is for those who have riches to enter the kingdom of God! For it is easier for a camel to go through the eye of a needle than for a rich man to enter the kingdom of God.""

We have read what Jesus said to the rich young ruler who asked Jesus what he should do to inherit eternal life. From his youth, the rich young ruler has obeyed the Ten Commandments. Jesus told him that he would also have to sell all he had and distribute to poor and he will have treasure in heaven and was to follow Him. However, when he heard this, he became sorrowful because he was not willing to give up all his possessions. But in the case of Cornelius, the centurion, even though he was a man of authority, he humbled himself before God Almighty, giving him all the honour and glory. He prayed to God always because he knew that he could not do without God. I believe God sent His Angel to show him what he should do because of his faithfulness to God.

About the ninth hour of the day he saw clearly in a vision an angel of God coming in and saying to him, "Cornelius!" And when he observed him, he was afraid, and said, "What is it, lord?" So he said to him, "Your prayers and your alms have come up for a memorial before God. Now send men to Joppa, and send for Simon whose surname is Peter.

(Acts 10:3-5)

Beloved, honestly, when we fear God, instead of men, God will show us the way, even though we do not know what we need to do to be complete as a follower of Jesus Christ, as He did for Cornelius. Apostle Paul says in Philippians, *"Being confident of this very thing, that He who has begun a good work in you will complete it until the day of Jesus Christ."*

Do you know, during those days it was unlawful for a Jew to be with Gentiles? However because Cornelius was faithful to God, God told Peter to follow them But the Holy Spirit told him to go with Cornelius men because He has sent them to him. Peter told Cornelius in Acts 10:9 & 23.

The next day, as they went on their journey and drew near the city, Peter went up on the housetop to pray, about the sixth hour. Then he invited them in and lodged them. On the next day Peter went away with them, and some brethren from Joppa accompanied him.

(Acts 10:9 & 23)

Apostle Peter had the courage to follow them because of the vision of the two parties received. Apostle Peter was like Pope in this end time. Do you think it was possible to just see the Pope or invite him to your house? He has people under him to assist him. However, God was involved in this matter. Acts 10:28-29 says, "You know how unlawful it is for a Jewish man to keep company with or go to one of another nation. But God has shown me that I should not call any man common or unclean. Therefore I came without objection as soon as I was sent for. I ask, then, for what reason have you sent for me?"

While Peter thought about the vision, the Spirit said to him, "Behold, three men are seeking you. Arise therefore, go down and go with them, doubting nothing; for I have sent them."

(Acts 10:19-20)

Honestly, if God did not reveal to Peter about this matter, Peter could have sent his assistant because he was very busy. What I understand from this story is that God wanted Peter to feed them by His Word and for them to believe and to be baptized by water and the Holy Spirit.

> While Peter was still speaking these words, the Holy Spirit fell upon all those who heard the word. And those of the circumcision who believed were astonished, as many as came with Peter, because the gift of the Holy Spirit had been poured out on the Gentiles also. For they heard them speak with tongues and magnify God. Then Peter answered, "Can anyone forbid water, that these should not be baptized who have received the Holy Spirit just as we have?" And he commanded them to be baptized in the name of the Lord. Then they asked him to stay a few days.
>
> (Acts 10:44-48)

Ladies and gentlemen, take note that nobody knows when the hour shall come. Put your trust in

God and believe that He is Alfa and the Omega. Believe in His Word. Do not be a double-minded person. Do not be carried away with the things of this world.

The Scripture declared in Psalm 118:8-9, "It is better to trust in the LORD than to put confidence in man. It is better to trust in the LORD than to put confidence in princes."

> Thus says the LORD: "Cursed is the man who trusts in man and makes flesh his strength, whose heart departs from the LORD. For he shall be like a shrub in the desert, and shall not see when good comes, but shall inhabit the parched places in the wilderness, in a salt land which is not inhabited. "Blessed is the man who trusts in the LORD, and whose hope is the LORD. For he shall be like a tree planted by the waters, which spreads out its roots by the river, and will not fear when heat comes; but its leaf will be green, and will not be anxious in the year of drought, nor will cease from yielding fruit."
>
> (Jeremiah 17:5-8)

CHAPTER 11

JOSEPH USED HIS GIFTS

It came to pass after these things that the butler and the baker of the king of Egypt offended their lord, the king of Egypt. And Pharaoh was angry with his two officers, the chief butler and the chief baker. So he put them in custody in the house of the captain of the guard, in the prison, the place where Joseph was confined. And the captain of the guard charged Joseph with them, and he served them; so they were in custody for a while. Then the butler and the baker of the king of Egypt, who were confined in the prison, had a dream, both of them, each man's dream in one night and each man's dream with its own interpretation. And Joseph came in to them in the morning and looked at them, and saw that they were sad. So he asked Pharaoh's officers who were with him in the custody of his lord's house, saying, "Why do you look so sad today?" And they said to him, "We each have had a dream, and there is no interpreter of it." So Joseph said to them, "Do not interpretations belong to God? Tell them to me, please." Then the chief butler told his dream to Joseph, and said to him, "Behold, in my dream a vine was before me, and in the vine were three branches; it was as though it budded, its blossoms shot forth, and its clusters brought forth ripe grapes. Then Pharaoh's cup was in my hand; and I took the grapes and pressed them into Pharaoh's cup, and placed the cup in Pharaoh's hand." And Joseph said to him, "This is the interpretation of it: The three branches are three days. Now within three days Pharaoh will lift up your head and restore you to your place, and you will put Pharaoh's cup in his hand according to the former manner, when you were his butler. But remember me when it is well with you, and please show kindness to me; make mention of me to Pharaoh, and get me out of this house. For indeed I was stolen away from the land of the Hebrews; and also I have done nothing here that they should put me into the dungeon." When the chief baker saw that the interpretation was good, he said to Joseph, "I also was in my dream, and there were three white baskets on my head.

(Genesis 40:1-16)

Even while he was in prison, Joseph continued to use his gift. Do you remember to use your gift while you were in prison? Beloved, I have a story to tell you. Once upon a time, there was a pair of twin brothers who were in jail. They were supposed to be released on Monday the following week they could not wait to be released. If they were to pay their fine, they could be released on Friday before the end of the week. One of the brothers told his brother that he had an uneasy feeling and suggested to his brother to wait till Monday to be released. But his brother did not want to spend another day in jail and was unwilling to wait till Monday. To make the story short, the brother who would not wait was released from prison first. On the same day he was released from prison, he got into an accident and died.

But remember me when it is well with you, and please show kindness to me; make mention of me to Pharaoh, and get me out of this house. Then he restored the chief butler to his butlership again, and he placed the cup in Pharaoh's hand. But he hanged the chief baker, as Joseph had interpreted to them. Yet the chief butler did not remember Joseph, but forgot him.

(Genesis 40:14 & 21-23)

The chief butler did not remember Joseph because it was not the will of God. Beloved, there are certain times when it is not the will of God for us to be in a hurry to get out of the situation that we are in. I have a Nigerian brother who used to do the cocaine business. One day he was caught and was put in prison for thirteen years. Do you know that it was in prison, God called him into the ministry? Today, he is a pastor of a church. Do you know, if he had not been arrested and put in prison, he would have died a shameful death?

My brethren, count it all joy when you fall into various trials, knowing that the testing of your faith produces patience. But let patience have its perfect work, that you may be perfect and complete, lacking nothing.

(James1:1-4)

Blessed is the man who endures temptation; for when he has been approved, he will receive the crown of life which the Lord has promised to those who love Him.

(James1:12)

I have a brother in Nigeria who was put in jail. It was at the time when the vigilant group was killing people who committed any offence in my country. At about the same period, the vigilant group was looking for my brother. I did not know what crime he has committed. I went to bail him out of jail but he refused. He said that he would not come out until the appointed time. I prayed for him and went home. So, when he came out from jail, I asked him why he did not want me to bail him out of jail at that time. He told me that the vigilant group was looking for him. Do you know if he had been in a hurry to come out from jail, they would have killed him? But he used wisdom and settled with them before he came out. There are times we do not understand why we are put in a certain situation or put in isolation. It is during this time that we should draw ourselves even closer to God and put our trust in Him.

> Now it came to pass in the morning that his spirit was troubled, and he sent and called for all the magicians of Egypt and all its wise men. And Pharaoh told them his dreams, but

there was no one who could interpret them for Pharaoh. Then the chief butler spoke to Pharaoh, saying: "I remember my faults this day. When Pharaoh was angry with his servants, and put me in custody in the house of the captain of the guard, both me and the chief baker, we each had a dream in one night, he and I. Each of us dreamed according to the interpretation of his own dream. Now there was a young Hebrew man with us there, a servant of the captain of the guard. And we told him, and he interpreted our dreams for us; to each man he interpreted according to his own dream. And it came to pass, just as he interpreted for us, so it happened. He restored me to my office, and he hanged him." Then Pharaoh sent and called Joseph, and they brought him quickly out of the dungeon; and he shaved, changed his clothing, and came to Pharaoh. And Pharaoh said to Joseph, "I have had a dream, and there is no one who can interpret it. But I have heard it said of you that you can understand a dream, to interpret it." So Joseph answered Pharaoh, saying, "It is not in me; God will give Pharaoh an answer of peace."

(Genesis 41:8-16)

Suddenly, the chief butler was able to remember Joseph because it was the will of God for him to remember.

Then the chief butler spoke to Pharaoh, saying: "I remember my faults this day. When Pharaoh was angry with his servants, and put me in custody in the house of the captain of the guard, both me and the chief baker, we each had a dream in one night, he and I. Each of us dreamed according to the interpretation of his own dream. Now there was a young Hebrew man with us there, a servant of the captain of the guard. And we told him, and he interpreted our dreams for us; to each man he interpreted according to his own dream.
(Genesis 41:9-12)

What do you think Joseph must have felt when he was told that the Pharaoh of Egypt wanted him to appear before the Pharaoh? It was the Lord's doing, for it is not by man's might or by power but by the power of the Holy Spirit.

Beloved, Apostle Paul said in 2 Timothy 1:6-9, *"Therefore I remind you to stir up the gift of God which is in you through the laying on of my hands. For God has not given us a spirit of fear, but of power and of love and of a sound mind. Therefore* do not be ashamed of the testimony of our Lord, nor of me His prisoner, but share with me in the sufferings for the gospel according to the power of God, who has saved us and called us with a holy calling, not according to our works, but according to His own purpose and grace which was given to us in Christ Jesus before time began."

If Joseph did not make use of his gift even while he was in prison, he might not be exposed and brought before the Pharaoh.

Remember, at the beginning in Genesis 37:5-10 the Scripture says, "Now Joseph had a dream, and he told it to his brothers; and they hated him even more. So he said to them, "Please hear this dream which I have dreamed: There we were, binding sheaves in the field. Then behold, my sheaf arose and also stood upright; and indeed your sheaves stood all around and bowed down to my sheaf." And his brothers said to him, "Shall you indeed reign over us? Or shall you indeed have dominion over us?" So they hated him even more for his dreams and for his words. Then he dreamed still another dream and told it to his brothers, and said, "Look, I have dreamed another dream. And this time, the sun, the moon, and the eleven stars bowed down to me." So he told it to his father and his brothers; and his father rebuked him and said to him, "What is this dream that you have dreamed? Shall your mother and I and your brothers indeed come to bow down to the earth before you?" He was sold to the Ishmaelite merchants by his brothers because they were envious of Joseph.

> Come and let us sell him to the Ishmaelites, and let not our hand be upon him, for he is our brother and our flesh." And his brothers listened. Then Midianite traders passed by; so the brothers pulled Joseph up and lifted him out of the pit, and sold him to the Ishmaelites for twenty shekels of silver. And they took Joseph to Egypt.
> (Genesis 37:27-28)

He that endures to the end shall be saved. Heaven and earth shall pass away but the word of God will not pass away.

CHAPTER 12

PAUL AND BARNABAS

꧁꧂

Immediately he preached the Christ in the synagogues, that He is the Son of God. Then all who heard were amazed, and said, "Is this not he who destroyed those who called on this name in Jerusalem, and has come here for that purpose, so that he might bring them bound to the chief priests?" But Saul increased all the more in strength, and confounded the Jews who dwelt in Damascus, proving that this Jesus is the Christ. Now after many days were past, the Jews plotted to kill him. But their plot became known to Saul. And they watched the gates day and night, to kill him. Then the disciples took him by night and let him down through the wall in a large basket. And when Saul had come to Jerusalem, he tried to join the disciples; but

they were all afraid of him, and did not believe that he was a disciple. But Barnabas took him and brought him to the apostles. And he declared to them how he had seen the Lord on the road, and that He had spoken to him, and how he had preached boldly at Damascus in the name of Jesus. So he was with them at Jerusalem, coming in and going out.
(Acts 9:20-28)

Beloved, do not love the things of this world. Picture this in your mind. Saul had a very bad reputation for persecuting those who believed in Jesus Christ. However, after his encounter with Jesus Christ while on his way to Damascus, his life was changed.

Then all who heard were amazed, and said, "Is this not he who destroyed those who called on this name in Jerusalem, and has come here for that purpose, so that he might bring them bound to the chief priests?" But Saul increased all the more in strength, and confounded the Jews who dwelt in Damascus, proving that this Jesus is the Christ."
(Acts 9:21-22)

All who saw him and heard his preaching were amazed because they recognized him as the person who destroyed those who believe in Jesus. But he did not give up, rather he increased all the more in strength so that the devil would be put to shame. I discovered that Barnabas saw him preaching to the people and also witnessed his sincerity and honesty. That was why Barnabas took the courage and brought Saul to meet with the apostles.

But Barnabas took him and brought him to the apostles. And he declared to them how he had seen the Lord on the road, and that He had spoken to him, and how he had preached boldly at Damascus in the name of Jesus.
(Acts 9:27)

But today, we do not expose the Saul's of this end time. Neither do we introduce them so that they would be known because of envy, even though we were meant to introduce them. Because of human mentality, we will not do so. I know of preachers who would keep silent instead of introducing them, whom God have brought before them. He would like people to praise him. But if people praise you and you are an enemy to God, as for me it does not make sense.

There was a little city with few men in it; and a great king came against it, besieged it, and built great snares around it. Now there was found in it a poor wise man, and he by his wisdom delivered the city. Yet no one remembered that same poor man.

(Ecclesiastes 9:14-15)

Do you know that God can still use you to expose somebody whom God has brought before you? I believe that when we testify about other's good deeds, God will see us through in Jesus mighty name. Jesus said in Mathew 5, "Let your light so shine before men, that they may see your good works and glorify your Father in heaven."

When a man's ways please the LORD, He makes even his enemies to be at peace with him.
(Proverbs 16:7)

If Barnabas had not introduced Paul to the apostles and told them about the miraculous things God was doing through Paul and also about his boldness to preach the gospel, God who called Paul into the ministry would still expose him. He could use someone else to do it. But it was meant for Barnabas to do so and that was why Barnabas became known as a son of encouragement and later God promoted him to be an apostle.

And Joses, who was also named Barnabas by the apostles (which is translated Son of Encouragement), a Levite of the country of Cyprus
(Acts 4:36)

Today, many have big churches. But there are many pastors who started with them and helped the church to grow, are not given the opportunity to preach in their church service. Remember, this world is very short.

For a thousand years in Your sight are like yesterday when it is past, and like a watch in the night.
(Psalm 90:4)

There are even preachers who owned the most expensive cars but those who are serving under them, whom God is using to set the captives free, will not even have a bicycle. There are also some preachers who are using their assistants to pray all night and to evangelize so that their church will grow. Still, no honour is bestowed upon them. How can this be? Ladies and gentlemen, let honour be given to those honour is due.

Let the elders who rule well be counted worthy of double honour, especially those who labour in the word and doctrine.

Timothy 5:17

CHAPTER 13

MY JOURNEY TO INDIA

❦

Then I heard the voice of the Lord saying, "Whom shall I send? And who will go for us?" And I said, "Here am I. Send me!"

(Isaiah 6:8)

Beloved, do you know that it is not easy to evangelize in India if you do not have money? Honestly, I discovered in India, the churches will only give you accommodation and food but 99% of the churches there will not give you any offerings. Instead, most of the churches in India will expect you to give to them after you have preached to the people.

He who receives you receives me, and he who receives me receives the one who sent me. Anyone who receives a prophet because he is a prophet will

receive a prophet's reward, and anyone who receives a righteous man because he is a righteous man will receive a righteous man's reward. And whoever gives one of these little ones only a cup of cold water in the name of a disciple, assuredly, I say to you, he shall by no means lose his reward."
(Matthew 10:40-42)

I could not believe it. Once upon a time, I went to India to preach the gospel and God really used me mightily. After delivering my message, I was given 300 Rupee by the pastor of the church I was preaching in. This same pastor came to Singapore and he was demanding that I should buy him a musical instrument. I had the money to buy the musical instrument but I was not moved to do so because he was pushing me to buy it for him. Rather, I took him to McDonald's restaurant and bought him some lunch and we ate our food together. I told him that I am living by faith. I gave him 1,000 Rupees but he was upset that I gave him only that much.

Remember this: Whoever sows sparingly will also reap sparingly, and whoever sows generously will also reap generously. Each man should give what he has decided in his heart to give, not reluctantly or under compulsion, for God loves a cheerful giver.

And God is able to make all grace abound to you, so that in all things at all times, having all that you need, you will abound in every good work. As it is written: "He has scattered abroad his gifts to the poor; his righteousness endures forever." Now he who supplies seed to the sower and bread for food will also supply and increase your store of seed and will enlarge the harvest of your righteousness.
(2 Corinthians 9:6-10)

Do you know that this pastor, who gave me the 300 Rupees, has many members in his church? Honestly, he could have given at least 1,000 Rupees or ask his congregation to give their contributions. But to my surprise, many preachers in India do not preach about giving because they were afraid to lose their members. How can it be? It is when we preach about giving, the Spirit of giving will be our portion.

I have preached in big churches in India. At times, instead of receiving an offering from them I would be the one who would give to them. It is time for us to learn how to give to the ministers of the gospel who preach in the church because our God is not poor. At one time, I preached in one of the biggest church in India that has about twelve thousand members. Whenever they asked me to come and preach, I would do so for several days. After I have finished my assignment, I was given 1,000 Rupees. I know that this pastor could have arranged to collect an offering from the congregation to give to me but he did not. It could be because he was afraid to drive his members away. It could be they only wanted their members to give their offering to them.

Do you know the same pastor asked me to build a church for him and told me that he would put my name as the sponsor for the building? I thought he was joking. Later, I discovered that he was serious. Apparently, many American preachers have come and built the churches for them and they believe that they cannot do it by themselves. Remember, Philippians 4:13 says, "I can do everything through him who gives me strength."

I went to Bombay to preach. I met the Bishop of the church in Bombay who gave me a place to stay and every week, he would host a meeting and he would invite me to preach. His meeting costs a lot of money. After the meeting, the people are treated to a buffet meal and everybody ate until they were satisfied. So one day, he announced to the congregation that there is God in India if we would only believe that our God is able to supply all our needs according to His riches in glory by Christ Jesus. I was amazed. To make the story short, as I was preaching in Bombay and in Pune, God used me tremendously to set as many captives free, in Jesus might name. I have preached in big churches and small churches. The biggest offering I would receive at the most is 1,000 Rupees. I am not preaching for money but according to the bible in 1 Corinthians 9:13-14 says, *"Don't you know that those who work in the temple get their food from the temple, and those who serve at the altar share in what is offered on the altar? In the same way, the Lord has commanded that those who preach the gospel should receive their living from the gospel."*

Even though I could be the richest man in the world, I have the right to receive an offering in any church that I preach. I remember preaching in a church in my hometown one day. After delivering my message, I was given an offering, but I refused to accept it. The man of God said to me that I was rejecting his blessings from God.

Do not be deceived, God is not mocked; for whatever a man sows, that he will also reap.
(Galatians 6:7)

I could not believe it. Immediately after he said that he tossed the money in an envelope into my car. Honestly, I was still a young preacher at that time. According to the law of the bible, when we give we will receive a double portion of blessing from God.

The pastor of the church in Bombay was very kind. On the first day, I met him he gave me some amount of money. After I have delivered my message he handed me an offering of 1,000 Rupees. By then God has spoken to me to go to Singapore. I did not know anyone there and I did not have the money to buy my air ticket to Singapore. So, after my message a small sized lady gave me her address and invited me to their house because her mother was going to hold a prayer meeting in their house. That day, I learnt that God can move His power any place He wishes if we would only obey Him.

If you are willing and obedient, You shall eat the good of the land;

(Isaiah 1:19)

So, during the meeting one of the ladies in the meeting asked me where I was staying and I gave her my address. The following day, she brought her uncle to meet me. I could hardly believe that God really knew my way about. The lady's uncle happened to be a millionaire and he was willing to pay for my train ticket to Bombay and my air ticket to Singapore. They took me to various places and had a good time together before I left for Singapore. If you want to have a divine connection from God, listen to what the word of God says in Psalm 126.

Shall We Pray

> When the LORD brought back the captivity of Zion, we were like those who dream. Then our mouth was filled with laughter, and our tongue with singing. Then they said among the nations, "The LORD has done great things for them." The LORD has done great things for us, and we are glad. Bring back our captivity, O LORD, as the streams in the South. Those who sow in tears shall reap in joy. He who continually goes forth weeping, bearing seed for sowing, shall doubtless come again with rejoicing, bringing his sheaves with him. In Jesus mighty name we pray Amen.
>
> Psalm 126:1-6

It Shall Come To Pass

And the dream was repeated to Pharaoh twice because the thing is established by God, and God will shortly bring it to pass. "Now therefore, let Pharaoh select a discerning and wise man, and set him over the land of Egypt. Let Pharaoh do this, and let him appoint officers over the land, to collect one-fifth of the produce of the land of Egypt in the seven plentiful years. And let them gather all the food of those good years that are coming, and store up grain under the authority of Pharaoh, and let them keep food in the cities. Then that food shall be as a reserve for the land for the seven years of famine which shall be in the land of Egypt, that the land may not perish during the famine." So the advice was good in the eyes of Pharaoh and in the eyes of all his servants. And Pharaoh said to his servants, "Can we find such a one as this, a man in whom is the Spirit of God?" Then Pharaoh said to Joseph, "Inasmuch as God has shown you all this, there is no one as discerning and wise as you. You shall be over my house, and all my people shall be ruled according to your word; only in regard to the throne will I be greater than you." And Pharaoh said to Joseph, "See, I have set you over all the land of Egypt." Then Pharaoh took his signet ring off his hand and put it on Joseph's hand; and he clothed him in garments of fine linen and put a gold chain around his neck. And he had him ride in the second chariot which he had; and they cried out before him, "Bow the knee!" So he set him over all the land of Egypt. Pharaoh also said to Joseph, "I am Pharaoh, and without your consent no man may lift his hand or foot in all the land of Egypt."

(Genesis 41:32-44)

Beloved, his dream did come to pass. That is why we need to wait upon the Lord until He will place us where we should be. Our God is Omnipotent God, who knows us even before we were born. Obedient to God's Word is a price to greatness and if we do not know the purpose of our lives, we cannot achieve anything in this world. Because of the pride of life, we miss our opportunity to receive the blessing of God.

I have not seen any preacher who has just started his ministry and became suddenly prosperous or become suddenly known to the world. We must start from the beginning. Remember that our Lord

Jesus started His ministry according to God's will. He was crucified at the age of thirty three years old. We know that he has a purpose and He accomplished it at the appointed time when He was crucified and on the third day, He was resurrected.

Therefore God also has highly exalted Him and given Him the name which is above every name, that at the name of Jesus every knee should bow, of those in heaven, and of those on earth, and of those under the earth, and that every tongue should confess that Jesus Christ is Lord, to the glory of God the Father. Therefore, my beloved, as you have always obeyed, not as in my presence only, but now much more in my absence, work out your own salvation with fear and trembling; for it is God who works in you both to will and to do for His good pleasure. Do all things without complaining and disputing.

(Philippians 2:9-14)

And the sons of Israel went to buy grain among those who journeyed, for the famine was in the land of Canaan. Now Joseph was governor over the land; and it was he who sold to all the people of the land. And Joseph's brothers came and bowed down before him with their faces to the earth.

Joseph saw his brothers and recognized them, but he acted as a stranger to them and spoke roughly to them. Then he said to them, "Where do you come from?" And they said, "From the land of Canaan to buy food." So Joseph recognized his brothers, but they did not recognize him. Then Joseph remembered the dreams which he had dreamed about them, and said to them, "You are spies! You have come to see the nakedness of the land!" And they said to him, "No, my lord, but your servants have come to buy food.
(Genesis 42:5-10)

Remember, Genesis 37:5 & 9 tells us, "Now Joseph had a dream, and he told it to his brothers; and they hated him even more. Then he dreamed still another dream and told it to his brothers, and said, "Look, I have dreamed another dream. And this time, the sun, the moon, and the eleven stars bowed down to me."

Joseph's brothers did not believe him when he told them about his dream, that he saw them bowing down to him.

There we were, binding sheaves in the field. Then behold, my sheaf arose and also stood upright; and indeed your sheaves stood all around and bowed down to my sheaf."

(Genesis 37:7)

Beloved, neither he that plants nor waters is anything, but God who makes the increase. Remember, Joseph was seventeen years of age when he was sold as a slave to Potiphar's house.

> This is the history of Jacob. Joseph, being seventeen years old, was feeding the flock with his brothers. And the lad was with the sons of Bilhah and the sons of Zilpah, his father's wives; and Joseph brought a bad report of them to his father.
>
> (Genesis 37:2)

Joseph was thirty years of age when he became the governor of Egypt. Genesis 41:46 tells us, "Joseph was thirty years old when he stood before Pharaoh king of Egypt. And Joseph went out from the presence of Pharaoh, and went throughout all the land of Egypt."

To make a long story short, it took Joseph thirteen years, going through the wilderness experience before his vision came to pass. Every believer of Jesus Christ will have to go through wilderness experience, if not the Spirit of God is not in you. The bible tells us in 1 Corinthians 10:13, "No temptation has overtaken you except such as is common to man; but God is faithful, who will not allow you to be tempted beyond what you are able, but with the temptation will also make the way of escape, that you may be able to bear it." James says, "My brethren, count it all joy when you fall into various trials. Blessed is the man who endures temptation; for when he has been approved, he will receive the crown of life which the Lord has promised to those who love Him."

Now Joseph was governor over the land; and it was he who sold to all the people of the land. And Joseph's brothers came and bowed down before him with their faces to the earth.

(Genesis 42:6)

Didn't Joseph's vision come to pass? We have seen that his brothers came and bowed down before him. There is something I learnt from this story. Joseph recognized his brothers but they did not recognize him. Ladies and gentlemen, even though the whole world would hate you, know that God loves you. John 15:16-20, 'You did not choose Me, but I chose you and appointed you that you should go and bear fruit, and that your fruit should remain, that whatever you ask the Father in My name He may give you. These things I command you, that you love one another. If the world hates you, you know that it hated Me before it hated you. If you were of the world, the world would love its own. Yet because you are not of the world, but I chose you out of the world, therefore the world hates you. Remember the word that I said to you, 'A servant is not greater than his master.' If they persecuted Me, they will also persecute you. If they kept My word, they will keep yours also."

CHAPTER 14

JESUS AND BLIND BARTIMAEUS

ತಿ೭

Beloved, it is not about your ability but rather, it is about your expandability for you to receive your healing from Jesus. I say to you again that it is not about your riches or about your size but it is about your boldness in prayer to hear from God. Do you know that there are many who are interested to come to Jesus but because of one thing or another, they could not bring themselves to do so? The story of Bartimaeus tells us that he was a man who knew how to turn his weakness into strength.

Honestly, it is not easy to see Jesus face to face and discuss about your problem with Him. But I believe what Jesus did was to release the word to the crowd or multitude and He draws the attention of those who needed healing. I hope you understand what I am saying. Blind Bartimaeus was a man of integrity who has been longing to see Jesus for a long time and when he heard that Jesus was passing by, he boldly lifted his voice strongly to draw Jesus attention so that he could receive his healing.

Then many warned him to be quiet; but he cried out all the more, "Son of David, have mercy on me!"
(Mark 10:48)

We have seen how he ignored the followers of Jesus and cried out even louder to Jesus even though they told him to keep quiet. Beloved, when opportunity comes, do not let opposition to take place. Rather, believe that you will overcome every opposition that may come your way. To my great amazement, blind Bartimaeus did not lose hope. Rather he believed that it was his day to be free from his problem. I also discovered that he believed that it was the appointed time for him to receive his healing.

Do you know that in those days, there could be others like blind Bartimaeus who did not believe that Jesus was the Messiah? Rather he could be like those who believe in the traditions of men. However, he must have heard that Jesus healed many people and believed that Jesus could set him free from his problem and healed him.

And throwing aside his garment, he rose and came to Jesus. So Jesus answered and said to him, "What do you want Me to do for you?" The blind man said to Him, "Rabboni, that I may receive my sight." Then Jesus said to him, "Go your way; your faith has made you well." And immediately he received his sight and followed Jesus on the road.
(Mark 10:50-52)

We have seen how he threw his garment and immediately came to Jesus and received his healing. As he threw his old garment away, he was casting away his old life and receiving a new life from Jesus.

I will greatly rejoice in the LORD, My soul shall be joyful in my God; for He has clothed me with the garments of salvation, He has covered me with the robe of righteousness, as a bridegroom decks himself with ornaments, and as a bride adorns herself with her jewels.
(Isaiah 61:10)

Blind Bartimaeus had a focus and a purpose. Do you know, when purpose is unknown, abuse is inevitable? Bartimaeus did not want to miss his blessing and because of his faithfulness, he received his blessing from Jesus.

Many have missed their opportunity in life. It could be in business, in ministry or financial break through or healing. According to the Scripture in Mark 10:47-50, "And when he heard that it was Jesus of Nazareth, he began to cry out and say, "Jesus, Son of David, have mercy on me!" Then many warned him to be quiet; but he cried out all the more, "Son of David, have mercy on me!" So Jesus stood still and commanded him to be called. Then they called the blind man, saying to him, "Be of good cheer. Rise, He is calling you." And throwing aside his garment, he rose and came to Jesus."

Blind Bartimaeus pursued his miracle and he was able to overcome every opposition or distraction from everyone around him. Verse 48 says that many warned him to be quiet but he cried out all the more. Beloved, if you want to have a divine connection from God, you must behave like blind Bartimaeus in every predicament.

Many people would gladly shout and lift up the name of their president or those who are in the dignitary positions. But when it is time to lift up the name of God to a new level and a new dimension, many will not give attention to it.

Beloved, heaven and earth shall pass away but His word shall remain the same. Honestly, when challenges come their way many will not exercise their faith in God. Rather, they will bow to the tone of the enemy. When we stand and face the challenges that may come our way, then God will manifest instantaneously.

When my father and my mother forsake me, then the LORD will take care of me.
(Psalm 27:10)

But the following night the Lord stood by him and said, "Be of good cheer, Paul; for as you have testified for Me in Jerusalem, so you must also bear witness at Rome."
(Acts 23:11)

Blind Bartimaeus' boldness and faith gave him the courage to bring the attention of Jesus so that he will receive his healing.

Shall We Pray

O LORD, our Lord, how excellent is Your name in all the earth, who have set Your glory above the heavens! Out of the mouth of babes and nursing infants You have ordained strength, because of

Your enemies, that You may silence the enemy and the avenger.

When I consider Your heavens, the work of Your fingers, the moon and the stars, which You have ordained, what is man that You are mindful of him, and the son of man that You visit him? For You have made him a little lower than the angels, and You have crowned him with glory and honour.

You have made him to have dominion over the works of Your hands; You have put all things under his feet, all sheep and oxen—even the beasts of the field, the birds of the air, and the fish of the sea that pass through the paths of the seas. O LORD, our Lord, how excellent is Your name in all the earth!

O LORD my God, I ask You to strengthen me so that whenever I lift up my voice to You, You will hear me as You did with blind Bartimaeus.

In Jesus mighty name. Amen.

CHAPTER 15

HEALING

⚜

Beloved, healing is the ability to believe and to confirm God's word in our lives. Through the word of God, we receive our healing. It is also the process of curing or becoming well. It is the process of curing somebody or of becoming well spiritually.

If you are not walking right with God, healing would not take place. Do you know that when there is no food to eat we would die of starvation? So, healing takes place in us when we eat well. It does not mean eating expensive food but eating food that will nourish us. I hope you understand what I am saying.

Now Jesus called His disciples to Himself and said, "I have compassion on the multitude, because they have now continued with Me three days and have nothing to eat. And I do not want to send them away hungry, lest they faint on the way." Then His disciples said to Him, "Where could we get enough bread in the wilderness to fill such a great multitude?" Jesus said to them, "How many loaves do you have?" And they said, "Seven, and a few little fish." So He commanded the multitude to sit down on the ground. And He took the seven loaves and the fish and gave thanks, broke them and gave them to His disciples; and the disciples gave to the multitude. So they all ate and were filled, and they took up seven large baskets full of the fragments that were left. Now those who ate were four thousand men, besides women and children.

(Matthew 15:32-38)

I am going to give a comprehensive meaning of the story of how Jesus fed the four thousand men.

Now Jesus called His disciples to Himself and said, "I have compassion on the multitude, because they have now continued with Me three days and have nothing to eat. And I do not want to send them away hungry, lest they faint on the way."

(Matthew 15:32)

What would you say if you happened to be in this situation and people in the multitude were fainting or died from hunger? Do you think that the ministry of Jesus would have stood? Honestly, every day in our lives is a healing.

Once upon time, I used to smoke Indian hemp, which is marijuana. I was living in the flesh. I would even smoke it and have no appetite to eat any food. Do you know that those who smoke that stuff will lose their appetite for food to give them nourishment and their minds become unstable?

So, the Scripture tells us that Jesus saw that the multitude was hungry and have nothing to eat because they have been following Him for three days. Jesus did not want to send them away for they might faint on their way.

His disciples answered, "Where could we get enough bread in this remote place to feed such a crowd?"

(Matthew 15:33)

Picture this in your mind. How would you feel when you are in a situation like this where you have four thousand people with you in the wilderness and they have been following you for three days and they have nothing to eat? His disciples did not know where they would be able to get enough food to feed the multitude because they were in the wilderness.

"How many loaves do you have?" Jesus asked. "Seven," they replied, "and a few small fish." He told the crowd to sit down on the ground. Then he took the seven loaves and the fish, and when he had given thanks, he broke them and gave them to the disciples, and they in turn to the people. They all ate and were satisfied. Afterward the disciples picked up seven basketfuls of broken pieces that were left over. The number of those who ate was four thousand, besides women and children.

(Matthew 15:34-38)

We have seen how our Lord Jesus proved to His disciples who He really is. I believe His disciples were observing what Jesus did and fed the multitude with the seven loaves and the few fishes they have. Beloved, do not think about what you will eat because David said in Psalm that those who put their trust in God shall be like Mount Zion which cannot be moved but endures forever.

They all ate and were satisfied. Afterward the disciples picked up seven basketfuls of broken pieces that were left over. The number of those who ate was four thousand, besides women and children.

(Matthew 15:37-38)

Do you remember, the story of Elijah? When he was in the wilderness, our Holy God fed him.

"Leave here, turn eastward and hide in the Kerith Ravine, east of the Jordan. You will drink from the brook, and I have ordered the ravens to feed you there." So he did what the LORD had told him. He went to the Kerith Ravine, east of the Jordan, and stayed there. The ravens brought him bread and meat in the morning and bread and meat in the evening, and he drank from the brook.

(1 Kings 17:3-6)

We have seen how God sent for the ravens to feed Elijah in the wilderness. Sometime later, the brook dried up because there had been no rain in the land. Then the word of the LORD came to him: "Go at once to Zarephath of Sidon and stay there. I have commanded a widow in that place to supply you with food.

(1 Kings 17:7-9)

"As surely as the LORD your God lives," she replied, "I don't have any bread—only a handful of flour in a jar and a little oil in a jug. I am gathering a few sticks to take home and make a meal for myself and my son, that we may eat it—and die." Elijah said to her, "Don't be afraid. Go home and do as you have said. But first make a small cake of bread for me from what you have and bring it to me, and then make something for yourself and your son. For this is what the LORD, the God of Israel, says: 'The jar of flour will not be used up and the jug of oil will not run dry until the day the LORD gives rain on the land.'" She went away and did as Elijah had told her. So there was food every day for Elijah and for the woman and her family. For the jar of flour was not used up and the jug of oil did not run dry, in keeping with the word of the LORD spoken by Elijah."

(1 Kings 17:12-16)

We have seen how God used the widow to feed Elijah and God also used Elijah to bless the widow and her son.

She went away and did as Elijah had told her. So there was food every day for Elijah and for the woman and her family.

(1 Kings 17:15)

If you want to have a divine connection from God, believe that God will use you in any situation you are in. Believe also that you can do all things through Jesus Christ who strengthens you. Do not easily give up.

Jesus Heals The Blind Man

Jesus answered, "Neither this man nor his parents sinned, but that the works of God should be revealed in him. I must work the works of Him who sent Me while it is day; the night is coming when no one can work. As long as I am in the world, I am the light of the world." When He had said these things, He spat on the ground and made clay with the saliva; and He anointed the eyes of the blind man with the clay. And He said to him, "Go, wash in the pool of Siloam" (which is translated, Sent). So he went and washed, and came back seeing. Therefore the neighbours and those who previously had seen that he was blind said, "Is not this he who sat and begged?" Some said, "This is he." Others said, "He is like him." He said, "I am he."

(John 9:3-9)

This is a wonderful story in the bible. Many are not willing to prove to the world that Jesus is really the Messiah. How can this be? This is a story of a man who was born blind.

Now as Jesus passed by, He saw a man who was blind from birth. And His disciples asked Him, saying, "Rabbi, who sinned, this man or his parents, that he was born blind?"

(John 9:1-2)

To make a long story, his parents did not want to acknowledge openly that their son was healed by Jesus Christ.

But the Jews did not believe concerning him, that he had been blind and received his sight, until they called the parents of him who had received his sight. And they asked them, saying, "Is this your son, who you say was born blind? How then does he now see?" His parents answered them and said, "We know that this is our son, and that he was born blind; but by what means he now sees we do not know, or who opened his eyes we do not know. He is of age; ask him. He will speak for himself." His parents said these things because they feared the Jews, for the Jews had agreed already that if anyone confessed that He was Christ, he would be put out of the synagogue.

(John 9:18-22)

Ladies and gentlemen, if you want to have a divine connection from God, let your 'yes' be yes and your 'no' be no. Do not lie or deny Jesus because of one thing or another.

I once watched a Christian movie one day. In this movie, there was a woman named Magdalene in the olden days. So those who were the anti-Christ asked her whether she believed in God. She said yes and the government passed a law that any man or woman who believes in God will be put to death. To my greatest surprise, as I was watching the movie, even though the woman knew that she would be killed, she did not deny her faith in God. So, she was put to death. When it is time for us to die and make it to heaven to be with God that is also healing. So, healing takes place in every area of our lives.

The man answered and said to them, "Why, this is a marvellous thing, that you do not know where He is from; yet He has opened my eyes! Now we know that God does not hear sinners; but if anyone is a worshiper of God and does His will, He hears him. Since the world began it has been unheard of that anyone opened the eyes of one who was born blind. If this Man were not from God, He could do nothing." They answered and said to him, "You were completely born in sins, and are you teaching us?" And they cast him out. Jesus heard that they had cast him out; and when He had found him, He said to him, "Do you believe in the Son of God?" He answered and said, "Who is He, Lord, that I may believe in Him?" And Jesus said to him, "You have both seen Him and it is He who is talking with you." Then he said, "Lord, I believe!" And he worshiped Him.

John 9:30-38

We have seen how Jesus found the blind man and healed him. Why did Jesus found him? It is because He knew that the blind man was not afraid of what he will go through; the challenges that he has to face, even though it would cost him to lose his life. He was willing to challenge the enemies of

God. When Jesus asked him whether he believed in Him, John 9:38 says, *"Then he said, "Lord, I believe!" And he worshiped Him."*

We have seen that God is concern where He is leading you. Honestly, God will not forsake you or forget you. He is the same yesterday, today and forevermore

CHAPTER 16

THE BENEFITS

❦

Beloved no man or woman knows when the hour shall come. The bible says in Mark 13:33-37, "Take heed, watch and pray; for you do not know when the time is. It is like a man going to a far country, who left his house and gave authority to his servants, and to each his work, and commanded the doorkeeper to watch. Watch therefore, for you do not know when the master of the house is coming—in the evening, at midnight, at the crowing of the rooster, or in the morning lest, coming suddenly, he find you sleeping. And what I say to you, I say to all: Watch!"

Jesus tells a story in Mathew 25:1-13, "Then the kingdom of heaven shall be likened to ten virgins who took their lamps and went out to meet the bridegroom. Now five of them were wise, and five were foolish. Those who were foolish took their lamps and took no oil with them, but the wise took oil in their vessels with their lamps. However, while the bridegroom was delayed, they all slumbered and slept. "And at midnight a cry was heard: 'Behold, the bridegroom is coming; go out to meet him!' Then all those virgins arose and trimmed their lamps. And the foolish said to the wise, 'Give us some of your oil, for our lamps are going out.' But the wise answered, saying, 'No, lest there should not be enough for us and you; but go rather to those who sell, and buy for yourselves.' And while they went to buy, the bridegroom came, and those who were ready went in with him to the wedding; and the door was shut. "Afterward the other virgins came also, saying, 'Lord, Lord, open to us!' But he answered and said, 'Assuredly, I say to you, I do not know you.' "Watch therefore, for you know neither the day nor the hour in which the Son of Man is coming."

Below is the comprehensive meaning to the word WATCH & HOUR according to the story of the Ten Virgins.

W   WAKE UP
A   ABIDE -ARISE
T   TESTIFY
C   CROSS-CROWNED
H   HOPE

WAKE UP

Then the kingdom of heaven shall be likened to ten virgins who took their lamps and went out to meet the bridegroom. Now five of them were wise, and five were foolish. Those who were foolish took their lamps and took no oil with them,
(Matthew 25:1-3)

What does it mean to wake up? It is the ability to make somebody realize something about themselves. It is to make somebody aware of what is going on and to rise up from the situation, It is to make somebody aware to become alert and active and to come out of our day dreams or thinking about something else that sometimes can be excessive.

James said, "Is anyone among you suffering? Let him pray. Is anyone cheerful? Let him sing psalms. Is anyone among you sick? Let him call for the elders of the church, and let them pray over him, anointing him with oil in the name of the Lord. And the prayer of faith will save the sick, and the Lord will raise him up. And if he has committed sins, he will be forgiven. Confess your trespasses to one another, and pray for one another, that you may be healed. The effective, fervent prayer of a righteous man avails much."

The story of the ten virgins tells us five of the virgins were foolish and the other five were wise. The foolish virgins did not have enough oil in their lamps. Verse 3 says, *"Those who were foolish took their lamps and took no oil with them."* Beloved, what do you think about the foolish virgins who did not have enough oil in their lamps? Do you know, this is what is going on in the churches today? Some will come to church with their bible and some will not. Some will give their tithes and offerings and some will not come with it. However, when they go to the restaurant they will spend a lot of money but to give God they find it very difficult to do so. Some will sing and give praise to the Lord when it is time to do so in church but some will not. Some will fast but some will not fast. Some will read their bible but some will not.

He who has clean hands and a pure heart, who has not lifted up his soul to an idol, nor sworn deceitfully. He shall receive blessing from the LORD, and righteousness from the God of his salvation. This is Jacob, the generation of those who seek Him, Who seek Your face. Selah. Lift up your heads, O you gates! And be lifted up, you everlasting doors! And the King of glory shall come in. Who is this King of glory? The LORD strong and mighty, The LORD mighty in battle Lift up your heads, O you gates! Lift up, you everlasting doors! And the King of glory shall come in. Who is this King of glory? The LORD of hosts, He is the King of glory.

(Psalm 24:4-10)

ABIDE AND ARISE

And now, little children, abide in Him, that when He appears, we may have confidence and not be ashamed before Him at His coming.

(1 John 2:28)

He who dwells in the secret place of the Most High Shall abide under the shadow of the Almighty. I will say of the LORD, "He is my refuge and my fortress, My God, in Him I will trust."

Psalm 91:12

Arise, shine; for your light has come! And the glory of the LORD is risen upon you. For behold, the darkness shall cover the earth, and deep darkness the people; but the LORD will arise over you, and His glory will be seen upon you.

Isaiah 60:1-2

Beloved, if you want to have a divine connection from God you must abide in His word, in every area of your life. In verse 4 it says, "But the wise took oil in their vessels with their lamps." We have seen that the wise virgins are the faithful ones in the church. They are those who know the God they worship. They are not afraid to come to church with their bible.

I have a testimony to share with you. When I was a baby Christian I always felt shy when I carry my bible to church because many people knew me too well because of the kind of life I used to live. However, my pastor discovered about it and he encouraged me to stop hiding my bible and carry it confidently with me. Ever since that day I never hide my bible again.

There is a benefit for not hiding our bible. Once upon a time in one of the African countries an armed robbery took place in a luxurious bus. The armed robbers were robbing from the passengers and they were shooting at many of the passengers in that bus. One of passengers who was with his bible began to speak in tongue when they shot at him but the bullets did not hit him. As soon as their bullets ran out, they fled the scene. If you want to have a divine connection from God then pray this prayer with me.

PRAYER

Shall We Pray

Be merciful to me, O God, for man would swallow me up; Fighting all day he oppresses me. My enemies would hound me all day, for there are many who fight against me, O Most High. Whenever I am afraid, I will trust in You. In God (I will praise His word, In God I have put my trust; I will not fear. What can flesh do to me? All day they twist my words; all their thoughts are against me for evil. They gather together, they hide, they mark my steps, when they lie in wait for my life. Shall they escape by iniquity? In anger cast down the peoples, O God! You number my wanderings; Put my tears into Your bottle; are they not in Your book? When I cry out to You, then my enemies will turn back; this I know, because God is for me. In God I will praise His word, In the LORD I will praise His word, In God I have put my trust; I will not be afraid. What can man do to me? Vows made to You are binding upon me, O God; I will render praises to You, for You have delivered my soul from death. Have You not kept my feet from falling, That I may walk before God In the light of the living? In Jesus mighty name we pray. Amen.

TESTIFY

The Spirit Himself bears witness with our spirit that we are children of God,
Romans 8:16

This is He who came by water and blood—Jesus Christ; not only by water, but by water and blood. And it is the Spirit who bears witness, because the Spirit is truth. For there are three that bear witness in heaven: the Father, the Word, and the Holy Spirit; and these three are one. And there are three that bear witness on earth: the Spirit, the water, and the blood; and these three agree as one. If we receive the witness of men, the witness of God is greater; for this is the witness of God which He has testified of His Son. He who believes in the Son of God has the witness in himself; he who does not believe God has made Him a liar, because he has not believed the testimony that God has given of His Son. And this is the testimony: that God has given us eternal life, and this life is in His Son. He who has the Son has life; he who does not have the Son of God does not have life. These things I have written to you who believe in the name of the Son of God, that you may know that you have eternal life, and that you may continue to believe in the name of the Son of God.

But while the bridegroom was delayed, they all slumbered and slept. "And at midnight a cry was heard, 'Behold, the bridegroom is coming, go out to meet him!'

Matthew 25:5-6

Do you know that Jesus is our bridegroom and we are his bride and whoever desires such an intimacy with Him, He beckons? Beloved, there is a need for us to testify about Him so that He will bless us mightily. To testify simply means to make a factual statement based on our experience. To make a factual statement based on personal experience or to declare something to be true from personal experience. To declare something that can be taken as evidence under oath in a court of law. To testify, religiously speaking is the ability to share God's words, deeds and actions. It is to declare the goodness of God in our lives and the wonderful things Jesus did for us. In the story of the Ten Virgins, verse 3 says this about the five foolish virgins, *"Those who were foolish took their lamps and took no oil with them."*

I will give a comprehensive meaning of the word OIL.

O   OBEDIENT
I   IMITATE
L   LOVE

OBEDIENT

It is the willingness to carry out what is demanded or ordered of us, particularly by somebody in authority. If you want to have a divine connection from God, you must testify about Him.

To the weak I became as weak, that I might win the weak. I have become all things to all men, that I might by all means save some. Now this I do for the gospel's sake, that I may be partaker of it with you. Do you not know that those who run in a race all run, but one receives the prize? Run in such a way that you may obtain it.

1 Corinthians 9:22-24

When we testify about His goodness, honestly, it is the greatest task He has commissioned to us. It is also obeying His word. Isaiah said, "if you are willing and obedient, You shall eat the good of the land; but if you refuse and rebel, you shall be devoured by the sword"; For the mouth of the LORD has spoken."

Ladies and gentlemen, let it be known to you that heaven and earth will pass away, but God's words will by no means pass away. And we know that all things work together for good to those who love God, to those who are the called according to His purpose. When a man's ways please the LORD, He makes even his enemies to be at peace with him.

Above all, the word of God says:

"Therefore do not be ashamed of the testimony of our Lord, nor of me His prisoner, but share with me in the sufferings for the gospel according to the power of God, who has saved us and called us with a holy calling, not according to our works, but according to His own purpose and grace which was given to us in Christ Jesus before time began"
2 Timothy1:8-9

IMITATE

Imitate me, just as I also imitate Christ.
1 Corinthians 11:1

It is the ability to mimic somebody or to copy the behaviour of somebody, voice, or manner, especially in order to follow somebody's example. It is also attempting to copy an existing method, style, approach or look alike. If you want to have a divine connection from God, listen to what the bible said in Hebrews 6:12, *"that you do not become sluggish, but imitate those who through faith and patience inherit the promises."* If you want to have a divine connection from God, Jesus said in John 14, "Most assuredly, I say to you, he who believes in Me, the works that I do he will do also; and greater works than these he will do, because I go to My Father. And whatever you ask in My name, that I will do, that the Father may be glorified in the Son. If you ask anything in My name, I will do it. If you love Me, keep My commandments. And I will pray the Father, and He will give you another Helper, that He may abide with you forever the Spirit of truth, whom the world cannot receive because it neither sees Him nor knows Him; but you know Him, for He dwells with you and will be in you. I will not leave you orphans; I will come to you."

LOVE

For God so loved the world that He gave His only begotten Son, that whoever believes in Him should not perish but have everlasting life. For God did not send His Son into the world to condemn the world, but that the world through Him might be saved. He who believes in Him is not condemned; but he who does not believe is condemned already because he has not believed in the name of the only begotten Son of God.

Ladies and gentlemen, how about those who believed in him but they are not testifying about His goodness? Jesus said in Matthew 7:25-27, "Therefore whoever hears these sayings of Mine, and does them, I will liken him to a wise man who built his house on the rock: and the rain descended, the floods came, and the winds blew and beat on that house; and it did not fall, for it was founded on the rock. But everyone who hears these sayings of Mine, and does not do them, will be like a foolish man who built his house on the sand, and the rain descended, the floods came, and the winds blew and beat on that house; and it fell. And great was its fall."

CROSS-CROWNED

And he who does not take his cross and follow after Me is not worthy of Me.

Matthew 10:38

Blessed is the man who endures temptation; for when he has been approved, he will receive the crown of life which the Lord has promised to those who love Him.

James 1:12

If you want to have a divine connection from God, you need to know the meaning of the cross.

> For He Himself is our peace, who has made both one, and has broken down the middle wall of separation, having abolished in His flesh the enmity, that is, the law of commandments contained in ordinances, so as to create in Himself one new man from the two, thus making peace, and that He might reconcile them both to God in one body through the cross, thereby putting to death the enmity.
>
> Ephesians 2:14-16

And the foolish said to the wise, 'Give us some of your oil, for our lamps are going out.' But the wise answered, saying, 'No, lest there should not be enough for us and you; but go rather to those who sell, and buy for yourselves.

Matthew 25:8-9

The story of the ten virgins is what is going on in the Church and it is just like those going to heaven and hell. Today, there are many preachers and the believers who know what is required to make it to heaven but because of their selfishness, they will not do it. There are also those who claim to be righteous only and nothing more. How can we live a righteous life if we do not carry the cross of Calvary?

How can we live only a righteous life if we do not attain the destiny He has set for us? Every believer is called by the Holy Spirit to do what God has set for us. *For many are called, but few are chosen.* However, many are carried away with the things of this world.

Apostle John said, "Do not love the world or the things in the world. If anyone loves the world, the love of the Father is not in him. For all that is in the world the lust of the flesh, the lust of the eyes, and the pride of life is not of the Father but is of the world. And the world is passing away, and the lust of it; but he who does the will of God abides forever. Little children, it is the last hour; and as you have heard that the Antichrist is coming, even now many antichrists have come, by which we know that it is the last hour."

I have fought the good fight, I have finished the race, I have kept the faith. Finally, there is laid up for me the crown of righteousness, which the Lord, the righteous Judge, will give to me on that Day, and not to me only but also to all who have loved His appearing.

2 Timothy 4:7-8

HOPE

Beloved, if you want to have a divine connection from God, seek first His Kingdom and His righteousness. I challenge you that God will see you through, in Jesus mighty name.

Therefore, having been justified by faith, we have peace with God through our Lord Jesus Christ, through whom also we have access by faith into this grace in which we stand, and rejoice in hope of the glory of God. And not only that, but we also glory in

tribulations, knowing that tribulation produces perseverance; and perseverance, character; and character, hope Now hope does not disappoint, because the love of God has been poured out in our hearts by the Holy Spirit who was given to us.
(Romans 5:1-5)

In Jesus name. Amen.

Below is a comprehensive meaning to the word HOUR.

- H   HONOUR
- O   OBEDIENT
- U   UNBELIEF
- R   RIGHTEOUSNESS

PRAYER

Shall We Pray

HONOUR

If you want to have a divine connection from God

Listen what Jesus said in John 5, "Most assuredly, I say to you, he who hears My word and believes in Him who sent Me has everlasting life, and shall not come into judgment, but has passed from death into life. Most assuredly, I say to you, the hour is coming, and now is, when the dead will hear the voice of the Son of God; and those who hear will live. For as the Father has life in Himself, so He has granted the Son to have life in Himself, and has given Him authority to execute judgment also, because He is the Son of Man. Do not marvel at this; for the hour is coming in which all who are in the graves will hear His voice and come forth—those who have done good, to the resurrection of life, and those who have done evil, to the resurrection of condemnation. I can of Myself do nothing. As I hear, I judge; and My judgment is righteous, because I do not seek My own will but the will of the Father who sent Me."

In Jesus mighty name. Amen.

OBEDIENT

If you want to have a divine connection from God listen to the word of God.

> Now it shall come to pass, if you diligently obey the voice of the LORD your God, to observe carefully all His commandments which I command you today, that the LORD your God will set you high above all nations of the earth. And all these blessings shall come upon you

and overtake you, because you obey the voice of the LORD your God: "Blessed shall you be in the city, and blessed shall you be in the country. "Blessed shall be the fruit of your body, the produce of your ground and the increase of your herds, the increase of your cattle and the offspring of your flocks. "Blessed shall be your basket and your kneading bowl. "Blessed shall you be when you come in, and blessed shall you be when you go out. "The LORD will cause your enemies who rise. against you to be defeated before your face; they shall come out against you one way and flee before you seven ways. "The LORD will command the blessing on you in your storehouses and in all to which you set your hand, and He will bless you in the land which the LORD your God is giving you. "The LORD will establish you as a holy people to Himself, just as He has sworn to you, if you keep the commandments of the LORD your God and walk in His ways. Then all peoples of the earth shall see that you are called by the name of the LORD, and they shall be afraid of you. And the LORD will grant you plenty of goods, in the fruit of your body, in the increase of your livestock, and in the produce of your ground, in the land of which the LORD swore to your fathers to give you. The LORD will open to you His good treasure, the heavens, to give the rain to your land in its season, and to bless all the work of your hand. You shall lend to many nations, but you shall not borrow. And the LORD will make you the head and not the tail; you shall be above only, and not be beneath, if you heed the commandments of the LORD your God, which I command you today, and are careful to observe them. So you shall not turn aside from any of the words which I command you this day, to the right or the left, to go after other gods to serve them.

(Deuteronomy 28:1-14)

In Jesus name, Amen.

UNBELIEF

If you want to have a divine connection from God, overcome your unbelief. Listen to what the word of God says.

> Blessed is the man who walks not in the counsel of the ungodly, nor stands in the path of sinners, nor sits in the seat of the scornful; But his delight is in the law of the LORD, and in His law he meditates day and night. He shall be like a tree Planted by the rivers of

water, that brings forth its fruit in its season, whose leaf also shall not wither; and whatever he does shall prosper. The ungodly are not so, But are like the chaff which the wind drives away. Therefore the ungodly shall not stand in the judgment, nor sinners in the congregation of the righteous. For the LORD knows the way of the righteous, but the way of the ungodly shall perish.

(Psalm 1:1-6)

In Jesus name. Amen.

RIGHTEOUSNESS

If you want to have a divine connection from God, listen to the word of God.

> Stand therefore, having girded your waist with truth, having put on the breastplate of righteousness, and having shod your feet with the preparation of the gospel of peace; above all, taking the shield of faith with which you will be able to quench all the fiery darts of the wicked one. And take the helmet of salvation, and the sword of the Spirit, which is the word of God; praying always with all prayer and supplication in the Spirit, being watchful to this

end with all perseverance and supplication for all the saints.

(Ephesians 6:14 -18)

In Jesus mighty name we pray. Amen.

EPILOGUE

※

And also if anyone competes in athletics, he is not crowned unless he competes according to the rules.
2 Timothy 2:5

Beloved, if you are willing to have a divine connection from God, you must complete the assignment He has put in you. Obedient to His word is a prize to greatness. If you do not know the purpose of your life you cannot achieve anything in this world. When we discover God's vision in our lives, God will manifest in us. God is willing to see His chosen vessels to do mighty things for Him.

> Now this I do for the gospel's sake, that I may be partaker of it with you. Do you not know that those who run in a race all run, but one receives the prize? Run in such a way that you may obtain it. And everyone who competes for the prize is temperate in all things. Now they do it to obtain a perishable crown, but we for an imperishable crown.
> 1 Corinthians 9:23-25

Beloved, do not give up. God has not rejected you. My bible tells me in Romans 2:11 that there is no partiality with God. Our God is not the author of confusion but of peace. God's word is settled in heaven. God's word never changes. He is the same God of yesterday, today and forevermore. Whatever assignment God has given to you, do it with all pleasure. Before God gives you an assignment, He has programmed all your activities till the day He calls you into His presence. I have not seen anyone who says that God has not exposed him; those who are willing to obey Him.

If you are willing and obedient, You shall eat the good of the land;

Isaiah 1:19

PRAYER FOR OBEDIENCE

Ladies and gentlemen, if you want to have a divine connection, then let us pray this pray.

Shall We Pray

"Now it shall come to pass, if you diligently obey the voice of the LORD your God, to observe carefully all His commandments which

I command you today, that the LORD your God will set you high above all nations of the earth. And all these blessings shall come upon you and overtake you, because you obey the voice of the LORD your God: "Blessed shall you be in the city, and blessed shall you be in the country. Blessed shall be the fruit of your body, the produce of your ground and the increase of your herds, the increase of your cattle and the offspring of your flocks. Blessed shall be your basket and your kneading bowl. Blessed shall you be when you come in, and blessed shall you be when you go out. "The LORD will cause your enemies who rise against you to be defeated before your face; they shall come out against you one way and flee before you seven ways. "The LORD will command the blessing on you in your storehouses and in all to which you set your hand, and He will bless you in the land which the LORD your God is giving you. "The LORD will establish you as a holy people to Himself, just as He has sworn to you, if you keep the commandments of the LORD your God and walk in His ways. Then all peoples of the earth shall see that you are called by the name of the LORD, and they shall be afraid of you. And the LORD will grant you plenty of goods, in the fruit of your body, in the increase of your livestock, and in the produce of your ground, in the land of which the LORD swore to your fathers to give you. The LORD will open to you His good treasure, the heavens, to give the rain to your land in its season, and to bless all the work of your hand. You shall lend to many nations, but you shall not borrow. And the LORD will make you the head and not the tail; you shall be above only, and not be beneath, if you heed the commandments of the LORD your God, which I command you today, and are careful to observe them. So you shall not turn aside from any of the words which I command you this day, to the right or the left, to go after other gods to serve them.

(Deuteronomy 28:1-14)

In Jesus mighty name we pray. Amen.

PRAYER FOR EXPOSURE IN THE MINISTRY

If you have been in the ministry for a long time and you feel that God has not exposed you yet, then pray this prayer with me.

Shall We Pray

Forever O LORD, Your Word is infallible. You are an awesome God. There is none like you. Your Word is settled in heaven O God. Your word says in Act 9:21-22, *"Then all who heard were amazed, and said, "Is this not he who destroyed those who called on this name in Jerusalem, and has come here for that purpose, so that he might bring them bound to the chief priests?" But Saul increased all the more in strength, and confounded the Jews who dwelt in Damascus, proving that this Jesus is the Christ."*

O LORD, I ask You to give me the grace to increase my faith in You. I ask you to give me the grace to enlarge my commitment in Your work. Use me O LORD to improve all the more in strength like Saul in the area of my ministry You have called me. Even though people are looking down on me, give me the grace to overcome and to increase all the more in strength in the ministry you have called me to hold. In Jesus mighty name we pray, Amen.

PRAYER FOR BARNABAS OF THIS END TIME

But Barnabas took him and brought him to the apostles. And he declared to them how he had seen the Lord on the road, and that He had spoken to him, and how he had preached boldly at Damascus in the name of Jesus.

Acts 9:27

If you want a divine connection from God to be a Barnabas of this end time, then let us pray this prayer.

Shall We Pray

Forever O LORD, Your Word says, "As iron sharpens iron, so a man sharpens the countenance of his friend. Be diligent to know the state of your flocks, and attend to your herds." Use me O LORD to expose others in the ministry. Give me the grace to be a Barnabas of this end time. Remove the spirit of envy from me and give me the grace to expose others, even though I am not yet exposed in the ministry. Give me the grace to expose others, if I am in the position to do so.

In Jesus mighty name. Amen.

ABOUT THE AUTHOR

Evangelist Innocent Mokwe is one of the Nigerian Men of God whom God is using mightily to spread His word in the world today. He is an international preacher who has travelled to many countries to preach the word of God and God has used him to heal many people during his evangelism and also used him to expose the work of the devil in the world and in the kingdom of darkness. He is a prophet with a powerful anointing of the Holy Spirit. His anointed messages have brought hope to many men and women of all ages.

He is also a prolific writer and has written many books. He hopes that many will be inspired by the books that he has written which would help the readers to strengthen their faith in Christ and in their daily walk with God.

Evangelist Innocent Mokwe was brought up in a Christian family. At the age of 12, he saw a vision of heaven. Heaven was exactly what the bible described, a place of paradise. He saw angels and the streets were paved in gold and the buildings were also made of gold. Everything was shining with glitters. It was breath taking.

It was during his college years that he began to mix with the wrong people and became influenced by his college friends. He started to smoke and drink and he would follow his college friends everywhere; even to pubs. He became weak in his faith and life became meaningless to him. After graduating from college, he went abroad to venture a new life. He continued to live an aimless life of smoking and drinking. Then in 1994, he was suddenly rushed to the hospital. All that cigarettes and alcohol and his reckless lifestyle have affected his health very badly. The doctors gave him several injections and caused him to sleep.

It was at the hospital while he was sleeping, he saw himself sitting on a chair and there were two angels holding him back from entering a tall iron gate. He saw another angel asking for his name and when he told the angel his name, the angel started to pray for him. He woke up after that and began to recover. God has saved him from death that day. His life began to change for the better and he became a new person. Life became meaningful to him and with God's help, he was able to drop all his bad habits. He no longer has any desire for the pleasures of this world. He began to have a personal relationship with God every day. The LORD told him to return to his country for a revival and so he went back to Nigeria and joined a ministry there and became an evangelist. Then he attended Pilgrim Bible College. He began to preach the gospel in his country. The LORD then told him to go and spread the gospel to other countries and led him to countries like Libya, Egypt, India, China, Cambodia, Thailand, Singapore, Malaysia and other countries.

For further enquiry you may send your email to:

evang632000@yahoo.com
imokwe63@yahoo.com.sg
mokeee1963@yahoo.com.sg
www.thelightofworld.com

LIST OF OTHER BOOKS WRITTEN BY THE AUTHOR

(www.thelightofworld.com)

- **JONAH GO TO NINEVEH PART**
- **TORMENTING PLACE**
- **ACCOUNT OF WHAT HAPPENS IN THE KINGDOM OF DARKNESS PART 1**
- **ACCOUNT OF WHAT HAPPENS IN THE KINGDOM OF DARKNESS PART 2**
- **DO NOT LOVE THE THINGS OF THE WORLD**
- **IS YOUR LIFE A LIVING TESTIMONY**
- **IT SHALL COME TO PASS**
- **MIXED IN THE MULTITUDE**
- **TRUE GOSPEL**
- **SPIRIT APPARENT**
- **SOLDIERS OF CHRIST PART 1**
- **CRUCIFY YOUR FLESH**
- **ARE YOU READY TO FARM FOR JESUS**
- **DIVINE CONNECTION**
- **WE ARE HIS MASTER BUILDERS**
- **BE SENSITIVE TO HIS DIVINE DIRECTION**
- **SEVEN STEPS TO SUCCESS**
- **IT DOES NOT MATTER**
- **ARE YOU A JEPHTHAH OF THIS END TIME**
- **THE BENEFIT OF DEATH**
- **JONAH GO TO NINEVEH PART 2**
- **WHAT IS YOUR MINISTRY**
- **WHAT IS YOUR VISION**
- **WAITING UPON GOD**

- ARISE AND SHINE
- DEEPER LIFE
- DOING GREATER WORKS FOR GOD
- WHAT IS YOUR PURPOSE
- SOLDIERS OF CHRIST PART 2
- DESTINY
- I AM GOING TO BREAKTHROUGH
- HYPOCRITICAL HOLINESS
- I SAW HEAVEN
- BE REDEEMED
- ABUNDANT GRACE
- HOW TO PURSUE YOUR GOAL
- ANOINTING
- SPIRITUAL MATURITY
- KINGDOM MENTALITY
- WE ARE ONE IN CHRIST
- WHO ARE WE TO JUDGE
- DETERMINING THE BEST SOLUTION TO YOUR PROBLEM
- PRAY UNTIL SOMETHING HAPPEN
- WHO IS YOUR HELPER
- COMPANION AND COMPASSION
- ATTITUDE
- HUMAN IDEAS
- MOTIVATION
- FEAR NOT
- MANAGEMENT ACTIVITIES
- SOCIAL INTERACTION
- EFFECTIVE GROUPS
- PRINCIPLES OF PARTICIPATION
- THE GOSPEL SHALL CONTINUE
- DIFFERENT KINDS OF PRAYERS

- CONFIRMATION
- THE FOOLISHNESS OF GOD IS WISER THEN MEN
- DON'T LABOUR IN VAIN
- MIRACLES
- UNDERSTANDING YOUR DREAMS
- THE GARMENT OF JESUS
- IS YOUR NAME WRITTEN IN THE BOOK OF LIFE
- THE APPOINTED TIME
- WORK OUT YOUR SALVATION
- THE STRATEGY OF DESTINY
- WORK OUT YOUR SALVATION
- THE STRATEGY OF DESTINY
- THE BENEFITS OF GIVING
- THE RAPTURE
- BE A PERSON OF INTEGRITY
- DISCOVER WHERE GOD HAS INSTORED YOUR BLESSINGS
- INCREASE YOUR FAITH IN GOD
- A LABOURER IS WORTHY OF HIS WAGES
- THERE IS HOPE
- ARE WE IN BONDAGE
- THE WORK OF THE HOLY SPIRIT
- A CITY SET ON A HILL CANNOT BE HIDDEN
- FULFIL YOUR MINISTRY
- THERE IS TIME FOR EVERYTHING
- THIS IS A FAITHFUL SAYING
- WHO IS ON THE LORD S SIDE
- WISDOM
- FOUNDATION IN CHRIST
- FEAR THE LORD
- DIFFERENT KINDS OF FAITH JONAH GO TO NINEVEH PART

- TORMENTING PLACE
- ACCOUNT OF WHAT HAPPENS IN THE KINGDOM OF DARKNESS PART 1
- ACCOUNT OF WHAT HAPPENS IN THE KINGDOM OF DARKNESS PART 2
- DO NOT LOVE THE THINGS OF THE WORLD
- IS YOUR LIFE A LIVING TESTIMONY
- IT SHALL COME TO PASS
- MIXED IN THE MULTITUDE
- TRUE GOSPEL
- SPIRIT APPARENT
- SOLDIERS OF CHRIST PART 1
- CRUCIFY YOUR FLESH
- ARE YOU READY TO FARM FOR JESUS
- DIVINE CONNECTION
- WE ARE HIS MASTER BUILDERS
- BE SENSITIVE TO HIS DIVINE DIRECTION
- SEVEN STEPS TO SUCCESS
- IT DOES NOT MATTER
- ARE YOU A JEPHTHAH OF THIS END TIME
- THE BENEFIT OF DEATH
- JONAH GO TO NINEVEH PART 2
- WHAT IS YOUR MINISTRY
- WHAT IS YOUR VISION
- WAITING UPON GOD
- ARISE AND SHINE
- DEEPER LIFE
- DOING GREATER WORKS FOR GOD
- WHAT IS YOUR PURPOSE
- SOLDIERS OF CHRIST PART 2
- DESTINY
- I AM GOING TO BREAKTHROUGH

- HYPOCRITICAL HOLINESS
- I SAW HEAVEN
- BE REDEEMED
- ABUNDANT GRACE
- HOW TO PURSUE YOUR GOAL
- ANOINTING
- SPIRITUAL MATURITY
- KINGDOM MENTALITY
- WE ARE ONE IN CHRIST
- WHO ARE WE TO JUDGE
- DETERMINING THE BEST SOLUTION TO YOUR PROBLEM
- PRAY UNTIL SOMETHING HAPPEN
- WHO IS YOUR HELPER
- COMPANION AND COMPASSION
- ATTITUDE
- HUMAN IDEAS
- MOTIVATION
- FEAR NOT
- MANAGEMENT ACTIVITIES
- SOCIAL INTERACTION
- EFFECTIVE GROUPS
- PRINCIPLES OF PARTICIPATION
- THE GOSPEL SHALL CONTINUE
- DIFFERENT KINDS OF PRAYERS
- CONFIRMATION
- THE FOOLISHNESS OF GOD IS WISER THEN MEN
- DON'T LABOUR IN VAIN
- MIRACLES
- UNDERSTANDING YOUR DREAMS
- THE GARMENT OF JESUS
- IS YOUR NAME WRITTEN IN THE BOOK OF LIFE

- THE APPOINTED TIME
- WORK OUT YOUR SALVATION
- THE STRATEGY OF DESTINY
- WORK OUT YOUR SALVATION
- THE STRATEGY OF DESTINY
- THE BENEFITS OF GIVING
- THE RAPTURE
- BE A PERSON OF INTEGRITY
- DISCOVER WHERE GOD HAS INSTORED YOUR BLESSINGS
- INCREASE YOUR FAITH IN GOD
- A LABOURER IS WORTHY OF HIS WAGES
- THERE IS HOPE
- ARE WE IN BONDAGE
- THE WORK OF THE HOLY SPIRIT
- A CITY SET ON A HILL CANNOT BE HIDDEN
- FULFIL YOUR MINISTRY
- THERE IS TIME FOR EVERYTHING
- THIS IS A FAITHFUL SAYING
- WHO IS ON THE LORD S SIDE
- WISDOM
- FOUNDATION IN CHRIST
- FEAR THE LORD
- DIFFERENT KINDS OF FAITH

www.ingramcontent.com/pod-product-compliance
Lightning Source LLC
Chambersburg PA
CBHW071602080526
44588CB00010B/994